STAND FOR GOD

"Will the Defendant Please Rise?"
(Evidence for God's Existence)

RICHARD LONG

ISBN 978-1-68517-847-5 (paperback)
ISBN 978-1-68517-848-2 (digital)

Copyright © 2022 by Richard Long

All rights reserved. No part of this publication may be reproduced, distributed, or transmitted in any form or by any means, including photocopying, recording, or other electronic or mechanical methods without the prior written permission of the publisher. For permission requests, solicit the publisher via the address below.

Christian Faith Publishing
832 Park Avenue
Meadville, PA 16335
www.christianfaithpublishing.com

Printed in the United States of America

ACKNOWLEDGMENTS

Thank you to everyone who helped contribute to this book (even the ones who didn't realize they were contributing). Thanks to my wife who has always stood behind me, encouraged me to write this book and to follow God's plan for my life. Of course, I also want to thank you for your interest in Christian apologetics. What is apologetics/an apologist? The word *apologetics* is derived from the Greek word *apologia*. Apologia means to defend. In 1 Peter 3:15, the Bible says, "Always be prepared to give a defense to everyone who asks you to give the reason for the hope that you have. But do this with gentleness and respect." Without apologetics, all we have to share with others about God and Jesus is our faith and personal experiences we have with God. Although that's enough for us, apologetics helps us to reach others who don't have faith, haven't had personal experiences, and it backs up our claims of why we believe what we believe in God and Jesus of Nazareth. We use philosophy, cosmology, science, physics, archeology, historical testimony, and known laws as evidence for our beliefs. I hope you find this book insightful, helpful, and encourages you to have the confidence all Christians need to have in order to talk about our faith in God and Jesus Christ to the entire world. God bless.

INTRODUCTION

Have you ever wondered, *How can we know beyond a shadow of a doubt that God and Jesus actually exist?* Far beyond personal experiences or by simply having faith can we truly know that They exist? Is there any hardcore evidence that we can rely on? Does what science teaches us really prove that there is no God and Jesus of Nazareth really wasn't who He claimed to be or was raised from the dead? These questions aren't unusual and are asked more often than not by Christians, other religions, and atheists alike. The biggest question and the most debated subject between scientists, atheists, and Christians is the origins of the universe and the origins of life. What it really boils down to is, does God exist, and how can we know for sure? What if I told you that we have evidence supporting both possibilities (a God/no God)? But which one is right? We have scientists telling us the universe is 13.8 billion years old, and the earth is 4.5 billion years old, and then we have the Bible "seeming" to tell us that everything was created in a six-day period. So which one is right? What should we believe?

Astrophysicist Karel Schrijver, at Lockheed Martin Solar and Astrophysics Laboratory, and his wife, Iris Schrijver, professor of pathology at Stanford University tell us, "Everything in the universe and on Earth originated from stardust, and it continually floats through us even to this day. It directly connects us to the universe, rebuilding our bodies over and over again throughout our lifetimes." On the other hand, the Bible says we were created in the image of God. As you can see, there is evidently several different topics and completely different views on the origins of the universe, our earth, and the origins of life. What I want to do is look into *all* the evidence science has to provide, dive into the evidence from philosophy, astronomy, cosmology, teleology, archeology, physics, and eyewitness testimony, and allow you to come to your own conclusion of whether or not the evidence points to a lucky coincidence/chance or if it was created through a perfect intelligent design by the God of the Bible.

Keep in mind, the evidence discussed is not 100 percent proof of one viewpoint or the other. What the evidence does do, is give the most logical, reasonable, and simplest answer for the events. This is what is known as Occam's razor. It is up to you to determine what that more logical probability is. I have studied many things, and have earned a Doctorate in Divinity, many theology certifications, Christian apologetics certifications, and have become an ordained minister. I have studied other religions, philosophies, cosmology (not one who applies make-up, ladies), and astrophysics. I have listened to countless amounts of debates, lectures, and podcast debates concerning Christianity and Christian apologetics. I am by no means an expert in philosophy, cosmology, or astrophysics. I don't believe anyone needs to be an expert in any field to follow the evidence provided by science to the most logical reasonable conclusion.

I have written this book for those who are not experts and may not understand all the logistics of science, so we can all comprehend what is being said so that way we can conclude where the evidence leads us. Apologetics is not a tool used to convert non-Christians to Christianity, but rather a tool used for defending the faith that Christians have in them. Also, as an apologist, I am here to put a rock in someone's shoe, making them uncomfortable with their thoughts and religion and hope it leads to them researching their own beliefs and coming up with their own conclusions. If after reading this book, and you decide the best evidence to you is to not believe in a God, that's okay. God has given us all free will, and you have the right to choose what you want to believe. But if after reading this book, you decide you have more questions or want more information to help you make a decision, my e-mail is on the back cover, and I will do my best to personally respond in a timely manner. Thank you for your interest in Christian apologetics. If you enjoy this book, you can join us on one of our social media platforms or on our podcast channel. God bless.

- iTunes: https://podcasts.apple.com/us/podcast/the-christian-apologist/id1544084684
- Spotify: https://open.spotify.com/show/2UEftPOOQ1dhdLwABfX6O9?si=LEGnOpjeRIiL6TCa_QKjGQ
- Google Play: https://podcasts.google.com?feed=aHR0cHM6Ly9hbmNob3IuZm0vcy80MjQwYWMwOC9wb2RjYXN0L3Jzcw%3D%3D
- iHeart Radio: https://www.iheart.com/podcast/269-the-christian-apologist-75440749?cmp=ios_share&sc=ios_social_share&pr=false&autoplay=true
- Stitcher: https://www.stitcher.com/podcast/the-christian-apologist
- Facebook: https://facebook.com/TheChristianApologist.org/
- Instagram: https://www.instagram.com/thechristian_apologist/
- YouTube: https://youtube.com/c/TheChristianApologist

THE BIG BANGER THEORY

Let us suppose you were to ask any high school student, or college student for that matter, how the universe came to be. There's a 95 percent chance they are going to tell you about the big bang theory. What is the big bang theory? Straight off the website *Phys.org*, it says,

> The basics of the theory are fairly simple. In short, the Big Bang hypothesis states that all of the current and past matter in the Universe came into existence at the same time, roughly 13.8 billion years ago. At this time, all matter was compacted into a very small ball with infinite density and intense heat called a Singularity. Suddenly, the Singularity began expanding, and the universe as we know it began and ultimately lead to life as we know it today.

The data from science has given us much evidence about the universe, and the scientist who analyzes this data should be teaching and exploring all the possibilities that the evidence points to with all the logical plausible explanations. Don't they do that already? No. Scientists like to use the term "Well, science tells us," or, "Science teaches us," when in reality science doesn't say anything. Scientists do. Considering the mass majority of scientists are either naturalist, materialist, atheist, and/or agnostic. When interpreting the data they've collected, it's only natural for them to see things that will coincide with their own beliefs. In 1978, a singer named John Conlee sang a song called "Rose Colored Glasses," which is a great way for us to understand how scientists interpret things. They only choose to see things from their own personal beliefs and perspectives.

Philosopher Thomas Aquinas, born almost eight hundred years ago, put it like this, "Most men seem to live according to what makes sense rather than reason." Science data itself very rarely gives data for only one plausible explanation, and when it comes to something as big as the creation of the universe, I highly doubt that it gives only one here. Scientists should not be biased with this data, but they should consider all possibilities, whether it goes against their beliefs or not.

Almost all scientists, cosmologists, physicists, and atheists now believe the universe had to have had a beginning. See, for the longest time, scientists had thought that the universe was eternal and had just existed forever. It wasn't until the last one hundred years did they really start to see the evidence of it not being eternal, but it had to have had a beginning. The universe having a beginning is a real problem for scientists, but we will get into that later on. Astronomer and publicly known agnostic Robert Jastrow agrees with the idea of scientists being biased on their conclusions of scientific data evidence by saying, "Scientists have no proof that life was not the result of an act of creation, but they are driven by the nature of their own profession to seek explanations for the origin of life that lie within the boundaries of natural law." When speaking of the big bang theory, physicist Alex Filippenko refers to it as the divine spark saying, "The divine spark was whatever produced the laws of physics. I don't know what produced that divine spark, so let's just leave it at the laws of physics." Instead of him just observing the data presented to him and admitting that there is a possible probability that there is a divine Creator, he'd rather ignore these facts and just leave it to what he knows best, physics. Scientists are still looking and searching for how the universe began. I personally agree with the scientific data science has already presented us, and that is the big bang. Yes, for all you Christians out there that don't believe in the big bang, I do. The difference between most scientist and myself is I know who banged it—God.

Travel with me back to the beginning, not the beginning of this book or this day, this week, this month, or even this year, but to the very beginning before anything existed, the beginning of the universe. Before the beginning of the universe, there was nothing. Absolutely nothing! Our finite minds cannot even begin to understand absolutely nothing. By even trying to understand absolutely nothing, we are using something (our minds) to try to conceive nothingness. Aristotle says this about nothing, "Nothing is what rocks dream about." In this wide array of nothingness, something came from nothing, or at least that's according to the late brilliant physicist, cosmologist, and atheist Stephen Hawking. So something came from nothing? In the scientific community, something coming from absolute nothing is a much more plausible explanation from the evidence given rather than something coming from an all-powerful being. Lawrence Krauss, another well-known physicist and cosmologist, who also happens to be an atheist wrote a book titled *A Universe from Nothing*; and in his book, he says, "The universe can come out of nothing without God." Now that just sounds like a lot of nonsense to me. Even if you choose not to believe in God, you can't possibly believe something comes from nothing. Could you? In the words of Professor John Lennox of Oxford University, "Nonsense remains nonsense, even when spoken by world-famous scientist." Albert Einstein's theory of general relativity says for anything to begin to exist, time, space, and matter have to come into existence at the exact same time. So for the universe to have been created by whatever means you choose to believe, time, space, and matter had to come together all at once.

In the early 1930s, through the 1950s, three scientists named Feynman, Tomonaga, and Schwinger reformulated the quantum vacuum. What's a quantum vacuum? *Quantum* is a fancy word that scientists like to use for describing the lowest possible energy containing no physical particles, and a vacuum is just like it sounds, a vacuum, except the pulling force is from gravity, not a suction from a powered motor. More recently, some scientists, such as Hawking, have been trying to prove something can come from nothing by using the quantum vacuum theory. There's a small problem with that theory though. What's that? The problem is even that claim is self-defeating because you are needing something (a quantum vacuum) beforehand to create your something out of nothing hypothesis/theory. Creating something out of absolutely nothing is an impossibility. Absolute nothing is literally *no-thing*. Wouldn't you agree? Therefore, we are left with only one practical logical theory, and that is an intelligent being created the universe. And that intelligent being has to be outside time (timeless), outside space (spaceless), and not made of material (immaterial). If it wasn't outside these realms, it, too, would have to have been created from time, space, and matter and would be constrained by these three things, just as we all are. The very first sentence of the Christian Bible points to this theory. "In the beginning God created the heavens and the earth" (Genesis 1:1). In the beginning (time), God created the heavens (space) and the earth (matter).

But what about when people say, "The universe is an infinite amount of space?" How many times have you heard that or been told that? The universe just goes on and on forever and ever. What if I was to tell you that there's plenty of evidence to prove that an infinite universe is completely false and inaccurate? Let's look at the evidence together. The word *infinite* is what we use to describe something our finite minds cannot comprehend. For instance, the speed of light is roughly 186,000 miles per *second!* That's extremely fast. In fact, that'll get you a speeding ticket anywhere you drive in the world. It's so fast we can't comprehend it. We can apprehend it, but we can't comprehend it, just like we can look toward the night sky and apprehend that the stars are in space but we can't comprehend everything that's in space.

The closest star to earth other than our own sun is four light years away known as Alpha Centauri A. Four light years away means it has taken four years from the light of this star to have been seen on earth, impressive but still imaginable. Let me break that down further. It has taken this light traveling 186,000 miles per second nonstop, 24 hours a day, 365 days a year for four years to reach the earth. In reality, I guess time travel does exist. How's that? When we see that star at night, we are literally looking at four years into the past. We are seeing what that star looked like four years ago. And that's the closest star to us! That'll give you brain freeze. The fastest mankind has ever traveled is 17,000–20,000 miles per hour or 5 miles per second, which is the speed of a space shuttle and the speed of the International Space Station traveling around the earth right this second. So if we were to head to the nearest star (Alpha Centauri A), other than our own sun traveling 20,000 miles per hour or 5 miles per second, 24 hours a day, 365 days a year, we would reach that star in roughly 80,000 years. That's a very long time. Now take into consideration that each star in our solar system is roughly 30 trillion miles from one another, and to travel from one star to the next at the rate of 5 miles per second or 20,000 miles per hour, it would take us approximately 200,000 years to reach it. Crazy, isn't it?

Do me a favor, keep in mind that distance and add in the fact that there are more stars in the universe than there are grains of sand on all the earth. With all the knowledge we have for the universe and earth, they estimate that if you take every grain of sand from every beach on earth and multiply it by one hundred thousand, that's approximately how many stars are in our galaxy! And now imagine that there are billions of other galaxies out there with their own cluster of stars. That is a lot of stars, and that's one massive universe.

Now think about this, without just one of those stars and the 30 trillion miles between each one of those stars, life could not exist on earth. How? The Atacama Cosmology Telescope (better known as the ACT team) in Chile and also the Hubble Space Telescope uses the oldest light known to exist in the universe known as the afterglow to date the universe. What is the *afterglow*? Afterglow is what scientists refer to as the CMB radiation that has been going through our universe some 380,000 years since the first formation of atoms after the big bang expansion. Scientists can see this afterglow and can determine the age of the universe. The universe, according to this method of dating, dates back to 13.8 billion years old. Now assuming the speed of light hasn't changed, which is an assumption (but a very good assumption because changing the speed of light will cause all other laws of physics to have to change, and therefore no science could be done at all), then the universe is 13.8 billion years old. So if the universe has an age, then that means that it has to have a beginning, which means the universe is finite, not infinite. Something that has a beginning cannot be infinite and finite at the same time. That would be breaking the laws of logic (the law of non-contradiction). Like Dr. Frank Turek says, "If the universe was infinite then, today never would've gotten here. There would always be another day before today."

Also look at it this way, every second that goes by is the end of time. If you think about that too long, it'll for sure make your brain hurt. The universe has been expanding at a great rate since the original big bang, but we now know that the energy from the universe is starting to slowly run down. How do we know that, and what does that mean for us? Through the studying of the second law of thermodynamics, we know that the universe is running out of usable energy. One of the many laws stated in the second law of thermodynamics says that "in all energy exchanges, if no energy enters or leaves the system, the potential energy of the state will always be less that of the initial state." Since the universe is losing energy, we also know that someday, we will go into what is known as heat death and destroy everything, including the universe itself. Don't be so quick to panic. This will for sure not be happening in any recent future. Scientists predict that heat death would occur sometime after 10^{100} of years! If something is really infinite, then it should never run out of energy. It should keep going and going and going, without ever running down like the Duracell battery Bunny. This also helps point to a beginning because since the universe is running out of usable energy, then it had to have had a starting point. The earth's age, on the other hand, is approximately 4.5 billion years old according to the scientific data. By using scientific methods such as carbon dating and radiometric dating, scientists have come up with the earth's age at approximately 4.5 billion years old.

Keep in mind, this is only assuming nothing has changed in this method of dating in the last 4.5 billion years. So how come a good number of Christians don't accept this data as factual? Well, a large number of Christians lean more toward the universe and earth being roughly six thousand years old. Why is that? In the Book of Genesis, it says God created everything in a six-day period, resting on the seventh day after He was done. So how do they get six thousand years out of six days? Well, the Book of Psalms 90:4 says, "A thousand years in your sight [referring to God] are like a day that has just gone by, or like a watch in the night." Also in the Second Letter of Peter 3:8, it says, "But do not forget this one thing, dear friends: With the Lord a day is like a thousand years, and a thousand years are like a day." So if we take that text in Genesis literally, then the six days spoken of in Genesis would amount to approximately six thousand years.

But let us examine the details of the text in Genesis a little more closely. The first verse of the Bible says, "In the beginning God created the heavens and the earth." So when did God create the heavens and the earth? In the beginning! It doesn't give a time frame. Now we can assume that the first verse was a prelude to the six-day creation, but once again, we would be making an assumption that we can't prove. What about the actual six days mentioned in Genesis? Well, let's look at those days. The first day doesn't begin until verse 3 of Genesis when it says, "Then God said." We also need to take a closer look at the word *day* used throughout Genesis, and we will see that there are actually four possible explanations for the word *day* in Genesis. In verse 5, God calls the light day and the darkness night. That gives us a twelve-hour period for the word *day*. Then in verses 11–13, God created all seed-bearing plants. Now I don't know about anyone else who might grow plants or vegetables, but even under the best conditions with super miracle growth, plants don't grow overnight. So we don't know how long that day actually was. Of course, we can say that God being all-powerful could've sped up the plant-growing process and made the plants grow instantly; but once again, we are making an assumption we can't prove. We also use the term *day* for many different meanings, such as "Troy Aikmen was a good quarterback back in his day." We aren't insinuating that he was only good for a twenty-four-hour period, but was good for his era.

Now in Genesis 2:20, God let Adam name all the animals. That's a lot of animals for Adam to have to name in a short twenty-four-hour period don't you think? In fact, there's a Christian comedian named Rob Bell who jokes of this and says when Adam started naming all the animals, he was full of energy. He was geared up and ready to go. "Woohoo, I get to name all the animals!" An animal would come by, and he'd say, "Rhinoceros!" Another would come by. "Hippopotamus!" Here comes another one. "Platypus!" and so forth. But by the end of it, Adam was out of gas. He was exhausted and drained. He was completely out of energy. Animals were still walking by, and Adam would say, "Ox, cow, dog." He was pooped! So the naming of all the animals would have to have taken longer than twenty-four hours. Lastly is the seventh day which we know is longer than twenty-four hours. How? Because it is the day God rested after He was done, and to this very day, we are still in that rest. So regardless of how one chooses to believe, whether the universe is old or the universe is young, we are having to make assumptions. One thing I can almost guarantee is that when we make it to heaven, God isn't going to be sitting there drilling us over how old we thought the universe actually was. It isn't going to matter. So far, evidence through science has given us two choices concerning the beginning of the universe—something came from nothing (the atheistic point of view); or it was created by a timeless, space less, immaterial, intelligent, personal being we call God (the Christian point of view). Let's keep digging into some more of the evidence.

The universe is also finely tuned for life to exist on earth. This is what's known as the teleological argument. We touched on it a little bit a few paragraphs back when we were speaking of the size of the universe and how all the stars would have to be where they are and the distance needed between them for earth to exist. So how's the earth existence finely tuned for life? Well, not only does earth have to be in optimal harmony for life, but so does the universe itself have to be exactly the way it is right now for life to have ever existed on earth. Let's first take a look at the universe as a whole. If Jupiter wasn't the size it is, with the mass it has, and the distance it is from earth, we wouldn't exist. Why? If it were any closer to the gravitational pull, it would suck us in. Any further away, earth would most likely be sucked in by the gravitational force of the sun, and if Jupiter was any further away, earth would be getting pounded by giant meteors and asteroids. Why's that? Jupiter is like a giant magnet, and thank God it is. Most asteroids and meteors get pulled into Jupiter by the gravitational force it has. These 16.5 to 65-feet-across meteors hit Jupiter on average one to five times a month. Some of these are equal to 100 million megatons of TNT! That's more than ten thousand times the world's nuclear arsenal in the height of the Cold War. Lucky for us, they never make it to earth. If you look at a close-up picture of Jupiter, you will notice hundreds, if not thousands, of craters across its surface. These craters are caused by asteroids and meteors that are the size of earth! When I hear of giant meteors headed to earth that can take us out, I'm rooting for Jupiter. Jupiter is my friend.

The gravitational force in space is so precise that if it was altered by one part in 10^{40}, that's a 1 with forty zeros behind it, the sun would not exist, and either the moon would crash into earth or would be lost in space. That's an extreme small percentage for this to have happened by chance. Let me give you a demonstration of this that I recently heard and think is a great representation. Pretend for a minute we could measure gravity by distance. Now measure from one end of the known universe to the other end. That's a long way! If the gravitational force on earth was dead center of that measurement and we moved it just one inch either way from that center point, life would not exist on earth. The universe had to have been created by design rather than by chance with those kinds of odds.

Now concerning the rate of expansion after the big bang, Stephen Hawking put it like this, "If the rate of expansion after the big bang had been smaller by even one part in a hundred thousand million, million, the universe would've recollapsed." That rate of expansion is why the average distance between the stars in our galaxy is thirty trillion miles! Just without that distance between the stars, life could not and would not be supported on earth.

Astronomer Robert Jastrow, founder of NASA's Goddard Institute and author of *God and the Astronomers*, on page 1, declares he's an agnostic. What's agnostic? An agnostic doesn't know if there is a god or not, but they're open to the idea of there being a God. But Jastrow then, on page 14, makes this astounding claim, "Now we see how the astronomical evidence supports the biblical view of the origin of the world. The details differ, but the essential elements in the astronomical and biblical accounts of Genesis are the same." In an interview, Jastrow also said,

> Astronomers now find they have painted themselves into a corner because they have proven, by their own methods, that the world began abruptly in an act of creation to which you can trace the seeds of every star, every planet, every living thing in the cosmos and on the earth. And they have found that all this happened as a product of forces they cannot hope to discover. That there are what I or anyone would call supernatural forces at work is now, I think, a scientifically proven fact.

He's saying that with all the evidence for the universe, earth, and the fine-tuning of it all, there has to be an external supernatural force that created it. Let's also take into consideration the tilt of the earth on its axis. Yes, even without the precise tilt of the earth, life could not have existed. The earth is tilted by 23.5°. If it was different by just a fragment, life on earth couldn't have existed. If the twenty-four-hour rotation of earth was altered, life would not have existed on earth. The earth is the third planet from the sun. This is what scientists call the Goldilocks zone. Why's that? If earth was any closer to the sun, we would burn up and any further away, we would freeze. We are in just the perfect spot to make life inhabitable on earth. It's clear to me that the universe has been precisely fined tuned for life to exist. Is all this by chance? Luck of the draw? These facts about the earth being so precise for life is what philosophers refer to as the anthropic principle. There are over 120 anthropic principles that we currently know of just about earth and it's fine-tuning to sustain life. We just briefly went over an extremely small amount for the fine-tuning argument, and there are over 120 more! We could talk about the oxygen ratio, the hydrogen ratio, the atmosphere, and the list goes on and on.

So was it all caused by chance? What exactly is meant when someone uses the word *chance*? *Chance* is a word we use to describe mathematical possibilities. Chance doesn't cause anything! *Chance* is just another word used by scientists to say, "We don't know." Is it by chance that the universe is so finely tuned that life's able to exist on earth? Absolutely not! How come? The other portion of the second law of thermodynamics helps to explain this. You cannot get order out of chaos. Think about this. The big bang was a massive expansion moving faster than the speed of light, close to that of an explosion without the actual bursting. An explosion is chaotic! How do we get order from disorder? We don't. We can't go blow up a skyscraper and expect the rubble to fall down and form a complete shopping mall with stores, light, walls, ceilings, tile, and a roof. If we aren't expecting those kinds of results from an explosion caused by intelligent beings such as ourselves, then how can we expect a much more detailed, finely tuned universe out of what atheists call a natural event? How is that even natural? If it was natural, then why aren't things just popping up out of nowhere? I'll tell you why. Because we know that things just don't pop up out of nothing without something creating it. If the universe and all that's in it popped up out of nowhere, how come we still don't see things popping up out of nothing? Is it possible a timeless, spaceless, immaterial, powerful, personal Creator (that being God) is responsible for the universe's fine-tuning? Absolutely, it's a possibility. And to me, it is a more probable logical conclusion based on known scientific data.

Another way to look at this is there are two types of causes: non-intelligent (natural) or intelligent. We can't say that a nonintelligent force caused the universe to happen and its fine-tuning because the nonintelligent force would have to be of nature, and we've already established there was nothing in the beginning, so nature wasn't here yet. Instead of even considering the overwhelming probability of the factual data that God was the Creator of all things, senior astronomer Seth Shostak at Search for Extraterrestrial Intelligence (SETI) thinks it's more probable that "the universe and everything in it could be a science fair project belonging to a kid in another universe." What? That's a probable explanation? Are you kidding me right now? Yet we consider ourselves intelligent beings? With those kinds of probabilities, how are we to trust our own logical thinking? I... I can't... I can't even begin... What? What was that again? Maybe I heard it wrong. Wow! Let us move on before I have a mental breakdown.

Everything on earth and in the universe seems to be moving in a specific direction. It is all moving forward. Different grass seeds move to become different kinds of grass, an apple seed moves to become an apple tree, cottonseeds move to become cotton, and so forth. Have you ever wondered what's telling that cotton seed to become cotton? What's telling the apple seed to become an apple tree? These seeds aren't in the ground trying to figure out how to become cotton or an apple tree. They just move that way. This is what we call the prime mover. Aristotle called it the "unmoved mover." He says that the entire universe and all that's in it is indeed moving in a specific direction. The force behind this movement is the unmoved mover (God). So tell me, what's the more logical and even probability for the universe to exist and all that's in it? What's a more logical analysis of all the data collected by science for the universes' fine-tuning? Chance? Luck? A science fair project from a fourteen-year-old in another universe? Or was it created by an all-powerful, timeless, spaceless, immaterial, personal, moral, intelligent God? Please don't say a science fair project. I don't think I could handle hearing any more nonsense like that. All the evidence listed is factual evidence that can be researched. It is through deductive reasoning we are able to come to the conclusion that there must be a God behind the creation of the universe, the earth, and all that is in it.

THE BOOK WITH NO AUTHOR

Everyone, at some point or another, has asked the age-old question, "Where did we come from?" I'm not talking about you and I personally, but life itself, the very first life. It had to come from somewhere. Some people say we're the product of millions and billions of years of evolution, the product of natural selection. The Bible says we were created by design from a designer and for a purpose, in the image of God. So which one is right? If your answer is evolution, I have an analogy for you to consider. Imagine you're walking down the street and came across a book. You pick up the book, and on examining it, you realize that no author was mentioned. Do you just assume it came together by chance? Do you assume that there is no author and the book just came together by natural processes? It would be the same as after a tornado ransacked a junkyard and coming across a perfectly built Lamborghini and assuming that through the chaos of the tornado, the Lamborghini was made. Sounds pretty ridiculous, doesn't it? That would be complete nonsense! You would obviously see the book and know that an intelligent being had to have written the book, just as you would look at the Lamborghini and know it had to have been built by an intelligent mind.

Here's another scenario. Suppose you were walking down the sidewalk, and a concrete company had just poured some new concrete. As you get closer to the orange cones placed there by the concrete company to keep people off the wet concrete, you notice there's an etch in the concrete saying, "Jason loves Sarah." You wouldn't assume that nobody put that there, would you? You wouldn't think the concrete just mysteriously formed that way or an earthquake shook the ground forming a three-word sentence. That would be ridiculous! You would know that an intelligent mind, most likely Jason, or Sarah wrote that in the wet concrete before it had time to dry. What I'm getting at is if we can know beyond a shadow of a doubt that an intelligent mind wrote a three-word sentence in concrete, how is it some people don't believe an intelligent being wrote the book of life (DNA)? Literally each one of our DNA strands are comprised of a 3.2 billion letter sequence in perfect sequential order. That is equivalent to one thousand encyclopedias, except all that is in just one single DNA strand! Just the odds of this happening by chance or natural forces and then forming with other strands on top of other strands on top of other strands two hundred times to form one single life-form is an astronomical mathematical impossibility! Yet most scientists and atheists believe that this is exactly how life as we know it began.

Charles Darwin discovered and wrote a book about evolution in 1859. Darwin was a naturalist, geologist, atheist, and a biologist. Even after he discovered the theory of evolution, which almost everyone accepts as truth, he later says, "The impossibility of conceiving that this grand and wondrous universe, with our conscious selves, arose through chance, seems to me the chief argument for the existence of God." Even the great Darwin himself doubted his own theory and couldn't even understand how his macroevolution theory could lead from a blob of cells to a conscious human being. This is what many apologists and Christians call the "goo to you by way of the zoo" mindset.

The majority of scientists today still believe humans are nothing but a product of macroevolution. "But hasn't evolution been proven?" Yes and no. What do I mean? There are two forms of evolution scientists refer to—microevolution and macroevolution.

What's macroevolution? Macroevolution is a theory that's never been proven but makes claims that over time, species will evolve into other species and holds claim that everything alive, including plants, bacteria, seaweed, humans, animals, etc., are all related and all came from the same blob. The majority of their claims come from the fact that human DNA is very similar to animals and plant DNA. Now

I'm no scientist, but even common sense tells me that if two dogs were to live for billions of years, they would never, under any natural circumstance, become a cat. For me, the more logical reasoning for our DNA being similar to other nonhuman DNA is because we were all created by the same Designer. Look at it like this. Someone that designs cups for a living will have the same basic design but with variations. Like we had mentioned back in chapter 1, astrophysicist Karel Schrijver says we're all stardust, and it was through macroevolution and billions of years of natural selection we get life as we know it today. How is that even logical? How is that reasonable? Scientists and atheists pride themselves on being the voice of reason, and yet their reasoning for the origins of life isn't even remotely reasonable!

Microevolution, on the other hand, I am a firm believer in. Microevolution claims that over time, species evolve but stay within the same species. For instance, a wolf over billions of years of evolution could evolve into a pit bull, a Chihuahua, a poodle, etc. But this form of evolutionary processes stay within the canine species.

Michael J. Behe wrote a book titled *Darwin's Black Box*. The book is of how Behe discovered that the intricate design of cells are irreducible because of its complexity, so it could not have evolved. This ruined Darwin's evolution theories for the creation of human life. Even now, scientists are trying to cling to the hope of macroevolution so much they are doing vast studies into epigenetic information to see if it's possible to change the structure of DNA to get a new body plan. With scientists being the voice of reason, they should know that the problem with this is DNA has its limits to genetic information. The human body is like a well-put-together computer. We don't assume computers came about by nature. Why would we assume that about human life? Doesn't make any sense, does it?

Bill Gates (founder of Microsoft), when asked about God, says he's "pretty much an atheist" and that the belief in a god "makes zero sense." He later makes a comment saying, "DNA is like a computer program but far, far more advanced than any software ever created." So let me get this straight. A man who's a genius, transformed the way the entire world runs things through computers also thinks DNA is like the most advanced computer program *ever* but denies there's a creator or designer for it? Instead of saying there is a God or at very least the possible chance for there being a God, he would rather say that DNA (a far advanced computer ever created) came together by chance or luck, or even perhaps necessity. I'm going to take a guess and say that if we start using the same logic as Bill Gates, we should also assume that he truly didn't create Microsoft, but it was just a product of nature and evolution and that Bill Gates is only claiming he created it. I wonder if that would make him upset if he didn't get the recognition of his own design, and people just assumed it was through evolution that Microsoft came about. How can someone like Gates, knowing how hard and difficult it was for him to create Microsoft, still choose not to believe that life (a far more advanced computer program) was ever created by design but rather it's the product of luck and/or chance?

But don't get too excited, Christians. Why? Because there is actually a slight "chance" that we did win the "luck" of the draw by evolving into humans. What? I thought we just discussed how it wasn't possible. I never said it wasn't possible, just not logical or probable. Yes, I'm sorry to inform all you, creationists, and God-fearing people; but scientific data does show that it is a possibility, not a logical possibility but a possibility nonetheless. The chance of even the very first protein molecules of life forming an amoeba in perfect order is one chance in 10^{164}. Wow! You're probably saying I can't even comprehend that large of a number. Yeah, neither can I. That's because what it's saying is there is only one perfectly ordered protein chain for every one hundred million, trillion, trillion, trillion, trillion, trillion, trillion, trillion, trillion, trillion, trillion, trillion, trillion failed attempts. That's eighty times more than the number of seconds that have passed by since the creation of the earth! That in itself should be proof enough. Why? How can we have all this life on earth when statistically we shouldn't even have one perfectly formed amoeba yet through natural selection? Now by us saying this actually could've happened still doesn't mean anything unless it happened over two hundred times and then somehow by "chance" came together through the forces of nature and formed any sign of life.

Two great physicists say that there are ten steps that must be taken for humans to have evolved from one genome. They claim that before this would've happened, the sun would stop existing, and the earth would've burnt up. Here is the mathematical equation they came up with: 4^{-180} to the 110,000th power, and 4^{-360} to the 110,000. So it is mathematically possible, just not a high probability and a much less logical way of analyzing the data provided. With these kinds of odds, many still hold firm that this is why we are here today. The most brilliant scientist today throughout the entire world have been trying to create DNA out of nothing but, even with all their intelligence, still fail at this attempt. How can they, being of intelligent minds, still not replicate DNA but expect DNA to have formed from no intelligent mind but by nature alone? They can't even do it themselves, much less have nature do it!

In 2014, Floyd Romesberg, a chemical biologist at Scripps Research Institute, says they have created a new life-form of E.coli out of scratch, and he was presented with an award for his accomplishment. The life-form he created was a combination of both natural and artificial DNA. So as they rejoiced over their amazing achievement, I can't help but notice that even their claim to creating life had to be made from artificial and natural elements of DNA. Let me ask you, "How is that creating new life?" That's not creating new life. That's simply modifying an already existing life. That's the same as a mechanic saying he created a completely new type of vehicle out of scratch when in reality, all he did was take the engine out of a perfectly good Ford F-150 and added it to a transmission he built by hand, using parts from the auto store and now wanting an award for his new complete design. Don't get me wrong. What they did took intelligence, precision, skill, time, and science; but it wasn't creating something new. It was the modification of something already pre-existing. I'm starting to understand Dr. Frank Turek's book *I Don't Have Enough Faith to Be an Atheist*. With just the number one to the 10^{164} alone would seem to take more faith for someone to be an atheist than to have faith in a Creator.

I've heard in many debates where people argue the design of the human body as not being perfect. What they're trying to say is "If God was an all-perfect, all-knowing, all-powerful being, then why aren't we living forever? Why didn't God create us with indestructible organs and veins? Why aren't we built more like Wolverine from X-Men, where when we get hurt, we just rejuvenate instantaneously?" I'm guessing here, but probably because it was never His intent that we live forever in these bodies on earth.

It's hard for anyone to question and complain about the design of something if we don't know what the intended purpose of the design is. It would be like me complaining that my MacBook is poorly designed because I can't control the electrical power grid in Los Angeles with it. It wasn't designed to control a power grid! It was designed to do more simplistic things, such as to write this book on. If God exists (and He does), then heaven and hell exist. So initially we never truly die, we just either move into God's presence (heaven) for all eternity or out of God's presence (hell) for all eternity. So if we aren't made to live forever in these bodies (which we aren't), the designer (that being God) achieved the purpose of His design.

People normally refute this claim and say, "But what about all the diseases people are born with? They weren't born perfect! Where's God's perfectly created designed body then?" First, I want to point out that making a claim of something being better and other things being worse is a moral argument. Why do I bring that up? Because atheists and agnostics can't use moral arguments due to them not believing in objective morality since they can't justify where objective morality comes from. They have subjective morality based on their own personal opinions. But we will get into that later on. For now, let's stick to the issue at hand. Just because a creator or designer of things makes something perfect for its intended use doesn't guarantee it'll come out perfect. What do I mean? Look at it like this. If I was to bake a cake, my purpose of this cake is to be devoured by my sweet tooth cravings. We all have them! As I finish making my beautiful, delicious-looking bundt cake, I place it in the oven and walk away. At some point, the thermostat on the oven fails, raising the temperature way above-set point, and my delicious Bundt cake is now a disastrous burnt cake. Now is that a fault of mine because my oven failed? No, of course not. It's a result of the oven failing.

The same is with God. He created and designed us perfect; but as He places us in a sinful, fallen world (due to our sins), sometimes flaws happen. All of us have flaws, we've all failed, and we're all sinners (Romans 3:23). None of us are perfect (Romans 3:10). We can't expect God's perfect design to stay perfect when it's placed in a fallen world. We're all born into sin. Don't believe me? Here's proof. Imagine placing three two-year-olds with full glasses of red Kool-Aid in a room with white carpet and leaving them unsupervised for a while. Foolish granted, but for the sake of this analogy or experiment, let's assume you did. I can guarantee one of them, if not all three, are going to spill their Kool-Aid. When you walk back in, you see the mess of your beautiful, white Italian carpet your wife handpicked from Italy. You're upset. You ask them who did it. Hearing the tone of your voice, they become fearful. At the same time, they all point to each other. Who told them to lie? Who taught them to lie? Nobody told them to lie, and nobody taught them to lie. It's natural for them. They were born into sin, and we all have a sinful nature. Sin is like poison to us. We can have someone who is in what we would call perfect health, but if they drink just small amounts of poison daily, they will get sick, and they will eventually die from it. This is why we need the great physician (Jesus). Our bodies are designed perfectly for the intentions of the Designer and for the intended purpose of our lives.

Biologists claim we are nothing more than millions, upon billions, upon billions of molecules, and nothing more (i.e., no spirit, no mind). If biologists are right and we are nothing but a bunch of molecules in motion, then that would mean every thought we had or are going to have is nothing but just random acts of molecules colliding, giving us what we conceive as our intellectual thought processes. That would mean that we don't have free will. Why's that? Because our brains would just be reacting out of responsive reflexes to what it knows from our past evolutionary process. Dr. Steven Novella, a neurologist from Yale, says the mind is an imaginary fairy and that only the brain exists.

Dr. Novella, like many atheists, is a materialist. Materialists only believe in what can be seen. If that is the true case, then how can we know what love is? How can we know what is good and evil? Here's what I mean by that. Knowing love and knowing good and evil isn't of the brain. They're volitional, emotional responses. Simply put, they're feelings. Feelings can't be seen or examined under a microscope. If materialists only believe in what they can see, then I guess materialists, such as Dr. Novella, doesn't believe in gravity either since it can't be seen. There is no love molecule or collision of molecules giving us love or the knowledge of good and evil.

It's impossible for materialists to know what those things are because it can't be seen. With that mindset, we couldn't objectively know anything but only subjectively. That would mean good and evil are just a matter of personal opinions based on the molecules colliding in each of our brains. One could only subjectively claim what Joseph Stalin did by killing millions of people was bad. It wouldn't be objectively wrong. It's just your opinion against Stalin's opinion. Don't get me wrong. This doesn't mean only Christians can know the difference between good and evil. We all know the difference. We are all born with a moral compass. The question isn't ontological (that we know morality), but epistemological (how we know morality).

We all know what good and evil is, right from wrong. The question is, how do we know what is good and evil? How can we justify morality without there being a moral law giver? There's not a good and evil molecule gene or cell running through our bodies, telling us what's right and wrong. We all know this because it's of our minds, and it's written in our hearts at birth (Jeremiah 31:33, Hebrews 8:10). We know good from evil because there's a perfect moral being (God) from whom we get the standard of goodness.

Did you know that every second that goes by our bodies are regenerating up to twenty million cells? Around one hundred million new red blood cells are created every minute. The human body is an amazing thing, definitely too amazing for me to say it's the product of an evolving blob. Considering some of the smartest people in the world, such as Hawking, Dawkins, Hitchens, Shermer, and many more, find complete satisfaction in believing and trying to prove that just our bodies alone could've evolved instead of being created is astonishing! We are also finely tuned to live on earth.

There are more theories than there is proof that we are the product of millions and billions of years of evolution. It's all just theories based on scientist interpretations from the data provided, in hopes of someday discovering it to be true. Richard Dawkins, one of the world's most leading atheists and evolutionary biologists, thinks of humans as "survival machines, robot vehicles blindly programmed to preserve the selfish molecules known as genes." Did you catch that? He says we have selfish molecules. I'd like to see that molecule under a microscope. I've never even heard of that before. For Christians to claim that there is a Creator, atheists, such as Dawkins and many more, want 100 percent proof of this, yet not even they can provide 100 percent proof of their own theories! When they don't have 100 percent proof, they say, "Give us more time, and we will prove it." I hate to be the bearer of bad news, but more time isn't going to prove macroevolution. It'll never happen. It's an impossibility, and it's the only theory they have to go on. But hey, I'm all for giving them more time.

Maybe in time, they'll see what all Christians already see, and that is there is a Creator and Designer for everything! When we don't have 100 percent proof of there being a God, they call it the "God of the gaps" argument. What is God of the gaps? Basically, what they're saying is when we can't find an answer to a question, we just plug God in to those gaps and expect others to accept it. Dawkins says this in his book *The God Delusion*, "Creationists eagerly seek a gap in present-day knowledge or understanding. If an apparent gap is found, it is assumed that God, by default, must fill it." The human species and the origins of the universe isn't a "God of the gaps" argument! We are using deductive argumentation from the same evidence as everyone else is seeing; and we are coming up with the most logical, reasonable, probable solution—and that's God exists!

Science has given more evidence for creationism than the macroevolution theory processes of us evolving from stardust to what we are now. Our brains being nothing but molecules in motion is not an answer to free will either. If our brains are nothing but molecules and there is no mind driving the thought process, then the molecules are only reacting to situations, not giving us the opportunity to exert free will. The molecules can only react to past evolutionary events. It also isn't an answer to the laws of logic or the laws of mathematics.

A famous Christian author and apologist William Lane Craig said, "Laws of mathematics and logic, morality, metaphysical truths, and aesthetic judgments are not a gene or product of evolution, or of the human mind. Even the scientific method of truth cannot be discovered." What he's meaning here by the method of truth is what physicists call the laws of logic.

So what are the laws of logic? There are three primary laws that make up the laws of logic: the law of identity (if I say it's raining where I'm at and if it's true then it's true), the law of excluded middle (if I say it's raining where I'm at and it isn't, then it's false). The law of noncontradiction (if I say it's raining where I'm at, it can't be true and false at the same time).

These laws would still apply even if no humans existed. How? For example, if the earth was empty and humans weren't here, would the statement "there are no humans on earth" still be true?" Of course, it's true! We don't need human minds to have the laws of logic. If nobody was around, would two plus two still equal four? Of course, it would because we don't need human minds to still have the laws of mathematics. These laws would still exist even if nobody was here. Why? Because these laws don't come from human minds, brains, or human concepts, but from the law giver—God. How can evolution create laws that weren't created by the human brain? It can't. It's impossible! Laws don't create themselves. They are created by law givers. These laws had to exist before we were created by the Creator.

In another book of Dawkins, he says, "DNA neither cares nor knows. DNA just is. And we dance to its music." In simpler terms, he's saying we don't have free will, and we can't act or think on our own. We're merely reacting to the dancing molecules colliding in our brains (like discussed previously). We are nothing but DNA molecules, and we have to dance to its music without rhyme or reason. I don't know about you, but my first initial question to his statement is, "Was that statement of his own thinking, or was that just the result of his DNA reacting/dancing to the music that was playing in his head at that time?" Michael Shermer another well-known atheist says this about the feeling of love,

> When I fall in love with someone my initial lustful feelings are enhanced by dopamine, a neurohormone produced by the hypothalamus that triggers the release of testosterone, the hormone that drives sexual desire, and that my deeper feelings of attachment are reinforced by oxytocin, a hormone synthesized in the hypothalamus and secreted into the blood by the pituitary.

I don't know about any of you, but I've never seen that in a Hallmark card. Gentlemen, whatever you do, do not ever, under any circumstance, give this as an answer when your wife asks you why you fell in love with her. It will not end well for you. But for people like Michael Shermer, love isn't an emotion. It's not spiritual. It's not a feeling. It's just a bunch of chemicals, molecules, and cells dancing and reacting to the music of their own DNA, giving them what they think is an emotional feeling.

A paper published in May of 2020 from Columbia University openly admits "Despite knowing when life first appeared on Earth, scientists still do not understand how life occurred." Well, would you look at that? Now we're finally getting somewhere. Scientists don't know how life happened! Hallelujah! And the truth shall set you free! Now is that an argument for Christianity? No, not really (an exciting confession nonetheless), but it does show that scientists don't have an answer to the origins of life no matter how hard they've tried or how bad they want to have an answer. This doesn't stop them from filling in the gaps with—dare I say it?—an atheistic gap, or better yet, an atheistic assumption? I don't know if that phrase has been coined yet but I'm calling the patent office immediately!

The human mind is very much real, though it cannot be seen, but most scientists don't agree with that. Scientists know we have brains. They can see and feel those, but they don't believe in the mind because it can't be seen. Gravity cannot be seen, yet we can see the effects of it, feel it, and believe in its existence. When it comes to anything, we must believe that before we can believe in it. What do I mean? Scientists first had to believe that gravity existed before they could believe in gravity.

There are two types of beliefs. How's that? There's believe that, and there's believe in. For example, I have to believe that my truck will get me to the supermarket before I believe in it getting me to the supermarket. First, someone would need to believe that God exists before they can believe in Him. To believe that God exists is easy when you follow the evidence given so far to the most probable, logical explanation. But to believe in God is up to each individual person.

So why are atheists completely okay with believing that humans are here by a lucky chance rather than choosing to follow the reasonable, logical evidence back to a Creator? Good question. Many will claim that it's because there isn't enough proof, or there's a lack of evidence to support such a God. Others will claim they just can't believe in something that sounds like a made-up fairytale, which is how philosopher AC Graylings puts it. We can have, and on many occasions have shown, more logical proof for creationism than evolution.

But there's a difference between proof and persuasion. Proving what the logical scientific data shows isn't the same as persuasion. So when somebody wants proof of God's existence, I'm happy to oblige. If they still choose not to be reasonable and recognize it as at least a plausible explanation, I walk away. Dr. Turek says it best by asking an atheist one simple question, "If Christianity were true, would you believe it?" Remarkably the answer I hear the most is about 50/50; 50 percent say yes, 50 percent saying no. That tells me that it's not a question of the mind being able to accept the evidence provided for God's existence, but a question of whether the heart wants to accept it. It's not intellectual, but volitional.

Many don't want to believe in God. Why? That's a good question. Some don't want to think about the penalties for their sins. They don't want to believe in an afterlife where hell actually exists. By the way, do you think people in hell want out of hell? Contrary to popular belief, not all people want to go to heaven. Why? Because not everyone wants to be with God for all eternity. And believe it or not, those in hell don't want out. How do I come to that conclusion? In Luke 16:19–31, it gives the parable of a man in hell that wants Abraham to send his servant down to him to give him a drop of water on his tongue and wants his servant to send a message back up to his brothers telling them about hell. Notice the man never asked Abraham or Jesus to be taken out of hell. He's not wanting out. He doesn't ask to be removed from hell. He's in hell still trying to bark orders at Abraham and his servant.

Thomas Nagel is a professor of philosophy and law emeritus. He says, "I want atheism to be true... It's that I hope there is no God. I don't want there to be a God." And yet he claims, "Conscious subjects and their mental lives are inescapable components of reality not describable by the physical science." In fewer words, his claim is physics can't account for consciousness. Atheist and writer Martin Rowson said, "If God proved He existed, I still wouldn't believe in Him. I don't believe in God not because I can't but because I don't want to." Not everyone wants to go to heaven even if they were persuaded and proven to be true. So even if they get to the "believe that" stage, they still refuse to "believe in" Him.

Lawrence Krauss, a theoretical physicist and cosmologist, also claims that we are all stardust and that the atoms from our left hand most likely came from a different star than the atoms of our right hand. Uhm excuse me? Not only does Lawrence Krauss expect us to believe that we came from stardust, but he also wants us to think that one side of our stardust bodies is from a completely different star than the other side? Yet atheists make the claim that we are the ones with a fictional mind. Krauss is then quoted saying, "Forget Jesus! The stars died so we may live." So let me get the facts straight. He and I both agree that someone or something had to die so we may live, but by me believing in Jesus dying for our sins so we may live is complete nonsense compared to his belief that stars had to die so we may live? And yet Dawkins says I'm delusional for believing in God. With all these brilliant scientists in the world, it's unsettling to me to think the best answer they can come up with is we're all stardust evolved from billions of years of natural selection into a no good, no evil, no mind or consciousness, colliding molecules dancing around to the music of our own DNA beings. Did I cover all of it?

Anthony Flew was one of the most famous atheist turned deist before he passed away in 2010. He was once quoted, saying,

> I now believe there is a God... I now think it [the evidence] does point to a creative Intelligence almost entirely because of the DNA investigations. What I think the DNA material has done is that it has shown, by the almost unbelievable complexity of the arrangements which are needed to produce life, that intelligence must have been involved in getting these extraordinarily diverse elements to work together.

Science data shows us that there are well over one hundred billion galaxies, all having their own planets, their own stars, and own moons. Many of these other galaxies are immensely larger than our own Milky Way Galaxy. And through billions of years of evolution just like on earth, not one single planet has had life originate through the evolutionary process or any process for that matter, as far as we know about it. I guess we are "lucky" in that retrospect. A lot of atheists are beginning to jump ship and are becoming deist and theist. What's changed? Did the evidence change? Did God change? Or have their hearts changed?

What happened was Occam's razor. What is Occam's razor? Occam's razor is when you are presented facts on two different ideas, and the simpler of the two is more likely correct. It's obvious which idea is the simplest to follow. They were at a standstill. They had nowhere to turn. Some atheists and scientists can no longer deny that the more logical, simpler probability for the universe to have been created out of nothing, and for humans to have been created is that there must have been a Designer who created all things and designed it with very fine precision.

THE GREATEST ARGUMENT FOR GOD

What is the greatest argument for the existence of God? Many Christians and many apologists have what they consider to be the greatest evidence for God. Just like all of them, I have my own as well. What is it? The contingency argument, also known as the Leibniz cosmological argument or the Leibniz contingency argument.

What's the contingency argument? Gottfried Leibniz was a German philosopher, mathematician, theologian, and scientist whose achievements included the invention of calculus. When speaking about the existence of the universe, he questioned, "Why is there something rather than nothing?" Why do we have a universe, instead of nothing? He asked this question because he endorsed the principle of sufficient reason. The principle of sufficient reason states if you take any feature of the world, if the world could have failed to be that way, then there must be some explanation of why the world is that way. In layman's terms, the contingency argument states that for anything to *begin* to exist, it has to have a cause. That cause is either by necessity out of nature or by an external force. So why did I make the word *begin* italicized? Because a lot of atheists like to claim that this argument could also apply to the existence of God. But this argument doesn't apply to God because God doesn't have a beginning. The contingency argument only applies to things that *begin* to exist. God is the uncaused first cause.

Here's how the contingency argument is laid out.

Premise 1: All things that begin to exist have a cause. Either by necessity out of nature or by an external force.

Premise 2: The universe has a beginning; therefore, the universe has a cause.

Premise 3: The universe was either created by necessity out of nature, or the universe was created by an external force.

Premise 4: Since nature didn't exist before the universe existed, the universe had to have been created by an external force.

Premise 5: Thus, the universe was created by an external force whom we call God.

Basically, what Leibniz did was further advance Aquinas's cosmological argument. I find this argument to be foolproof. What do I mean? Nobody can argue the fact that anything that begins to exist has to have a cause. There is 100 percent no way around this. Most scientists, cosmologists, and even the majority of atheist are now admitting that the evidence for the universe to have had a beginning is undeniable (minus a small few who are still trying to prove its existence from the quantum vacuum theories). If all things that have a beginning have a cause and the universe has a beginning, then there must be a cause. That cause is either necessity by nature or external force. There's no way around this. There's no loophole. There's no subjective reasoning to explain this. The next time you start having a discussion with an atheist, just ask them, "Why is there something rather than nothing?"

IS MORALITY JUSTIFIED?

Before we begin, we must define *morality* and what it is. Morality is the knowing of what is considered good and evil, right and wrong. An example of this would be killing is bad, and living is good. Morality is an ontological statement. What do I mean? Everyone knows what is good and what is evil. Everyone knows what is right and wrong. We've known this since we were children. We're also taught this at a young age. It's also known as the golden rule, and the Bible says that God's laws are written on our hearts from birth. So it begs the question, what is good? What is evil? Not literally wanting you to name all that is considered good and evil but asking for the epistemological side of the question.

How do we know what is good and what is evil? Where do our moral standards come from? Morality has to have a standard above us. If it doesn't, then it's no longer a standard but a subjective opinion. In Dawkins's book *River Out of Eden*, on page 133, he says, "There is no evil and there is no good." To Richard Dawkins what Adolph Hitler did or Joseph Stalin did wasn't evil. His statement is self-refuting. Why? By using that same logic, we can also say anything Richard Dawkins says isn't good either. So why should we be listening to anything he has to say? C. S. Lewis, who was once an atheist then turned Christian, put the idea of knowing good and evil best when he said, "My argument against God was that the universe seemed so cruel and unjust. But how had I got this idea of just and unjust? A man does not call a line crooked unless he has some idea of a straight line. What was I comparing this universe with when I called it unjust?"

If atheists are right and we are just billions of years of evolved stardust molecules, then how can we justify what is right and wrong? If we have no objective standard of good to look toward, then anything we perceive as good or bad is just our own personal subjective opinions. We have to have a standard beyond us for us to be able to measure what is truly right and what is truly wrong. When atheist make claims that God is immoral, what they're really saying is, this is why I hate God. But that's another chapter we will speak about later.

I had an atheist named Matthew argue this point one time, and he was convinced that we are all products of evolution. At the end of our talk, I asked him, "So which molecule, cell, or DNA strand is responsible for our morality?" His face went blank. He had no answer. This doesn't in any way mean atheists can't know morality. Atheists, like Christians, know morality. We don't need the Bible to know morality. This isn't a question of ontology (that being we know morality) but a question of epistemology (how do we know morality?). We all understand we know right from wrong, good from evil. I'm asking how atheists can justify morality? How can they justify how they know right from wrong? Christians can justify morality because we know that morality comes from the moral law giver, the nature of God. He is the standard of good. But for atheists who don't believe in God, where do they think knowing what is morally good and bad comes from? How can billions of years of evolution teach us what is right and what is wrong? Darwin says, "With me the horrid doubt always arises whether the convictions of man's mind, which has been developed from the mid of the lower animals, are of any value or at all trustworthy. Would anyone trust in the convictions of a monkey, if there are any convictions in such a mind?" If there is no objective morality of goodness, then burning babies isn't objectively wrong.

We couldn't say that Hitler killing millions of Jews, homosexuals, different ethnicities, and people with disabilities in the holocaust was wrong either. It would just be a matter of our opinion against Hitler's opinion. Hitler thought what he was doing was good for the human race. He saw no wrong in killing people to better humanity. If there isn't an objective morality of goodness, if there isn't a moral law giver, then Hitler wasn't in the wrong *objectively*. That's just your opinion against Hitler's or Stalin's or the attackers of 9/11 in New York.

There is nothing biologically or chemically inside any of us that tells us what's right and wrong. The reason we know right from wrong is from the moral lawgiver, and He placed these morals on our hearts. "I will put my law within them, and I will write it on their hearts" (Jeremiah 31:33), also in Hebrews 8:10, "I will put my laws into their minds, and write them on their hearts, and I will be their God, and they shall be my people." Biology and chemistry are descriptive in nature, not prescriptive. What do I mean? Biology tells us what is. It can't tell us what ought to be. Evolution can show us what *does* survive, but it cannot say what *should* survive.

In 1991, the world was in disgust by the actions that came to light of none other than cannibal Jeffrey Dahmer. Dahmer had killed seventeen people in a thirteen-year span, dismembering their bodies and keeping some of the body parts as souvenirs. This was a horrifically evil thing that had been done. Anyone who disagrees needs to be institutionalized. When Dahmer was questioned about his actions, he stated, "If a person doesn't think there is a God to be accountable to, then—then what's the point of trying to modify your behavior to keep it within acceptable ranges? That's how I thought anyway. I always believed the theory of evolution as truth, that we all just came from the slime. When we, when we died, you know, that was it, there is nothing." I'm not saying or claiming that all atheists are deranged lunatics like Dahmer was. Most atheists, like everyone else, have good moral values. But you can see how Dahmer justified his behavior by thinking he would never have to appeal to a morally just God. His killings were justified to him and only him. Nobody in their right mind would agree with what Dahmer had done (that's objective morality). This was his subjective opinion on what is right and wrong.

Atheists claim that morality is the process of evolution. So here's my question to atheists. Suppose morality is the product of evolution. If evolution, by definition, is the process of things constantly changing to make life better, then someday maybe rape and murder will be morally good. They'll say, "Those aren't good things. That doesn't help life flourish." Oh, but it does actually. How's that? Rape just helps to populate the human species, and murder helps keep the population balanced. So how again is morality a product of natural selection through evolution? I'm waiting. I'm sure that question will never be answered. Why? Because if they say no, then they're admitting not all things evolve. If they say yes, then they're showing that their logic is extremely flawed. Atheists like to say that doing good to others is good for the human species. They also say that prevailing in life means to not murder others and that in return helps the human species to continue to flourish. On the website *Athiests.org*, they say,

> Natural selection has equipped us with nervous systems which are peculiarly sensitive to the emotional status of our fellows. Among our kind, emotions are contagious, and it is only the rare psychopathic mutants among us who can be happy in the midst of a sad society. It is in our nature to be happy in the midst of happiness, sad in the midst of sadness.

It is in our nature, fortunately, to seek happiness for our fellows at the same time as we seek it for ourselves. Our happiness is greater when it is shared. Let's stop right there. Says who? Whose happiness is greater when shared with others? Hitler's happiness wasn't greater when others were happier. Stalin's happiness wasn't greater! These must be the excluded psychopaths they mentioned at the beginning of their statement. So for the sake of argument, let us assume that Nazi Germany would've prevailed and taken over the entire world, like Hitler was trying to do. If all of us were now raised with only knowing Nazi Germany mentality, would the innocent murdering of Jews, homosexuals, and people with disabilities be considered good then? Or would it still be bad? Atheists can't say what is considered greater happiness when they have no objective standard to compare it to. They are throwing around their own personal subjective opinions and assuming it's a one-size-fits-all.

Now some of what they say I can agree with. But there is a problem with their ideology. They use terms such as *happiness*, *greater*, and *being kind*. Where are they getting that happiness, greater, and being kind are good things? They are failing to provide proof of a good or happy gene, cell, or molecule. There is nothing inside us biologically that shows us what happiness and kindness is, or should be. For atheists, this is all just a matter of personal subjective opinions. Dahmer, Stalin, and Hitler didn't share the same opinion when it came to the murdering of innocent people. For them, happiness, greater, and goodness was the murdering of innocent lives. They believed they were doing a good thing. If you're an atheist, then your thoughts on what they did are just a matter of your opinion against theirs. When referring to something as being good, you need to have an objective standard above your own. If there is no objective standard, a standard to look up to, then it's just a matter of opinion.

When speaking to religions (Christians more often than not), atheists like to resort to Plato's "Euthyphro dilemma." What's the Euthyphro dilemma? Plato had a dialogue, and in the dialogue, Socrates asked Euthyphro this question, "Is it moral because God says so, or does God say so because it's moral?" This was a dilemma indeed for Euthyphro. Either way he answered would point to God not being a morally good God, or it would show that God needed to seek a standard above His own nature to know if it was considered good. Unfortunately, for atheists, Euthyphro's dilemma has been found to be a fallacy. Why? Because God is the standard of morality. He doesn't look to a higher power to know what good morals are when He Himself is the standard of such morality. The question asked by Socrates is presuming God has to look somewhere other than Himself for an answer to morality.

Atheists can ask Christians, "What is good then?" They can turn the same question around on us as we use on them. We have a short and simple answer to this. It's summed up with a philosophical notion of identity expressed symbolically as $A = A$ or $B = B$. When one thing is identical to another, there are not two things, but only one. So when Christians speak of good, we are speaking of the very characteristics of God's nature. There's not a difference in the two.

Moral arguments are some of the hardest for atheists to debate. Why? They have no means of recognizing where it comes from. They have no way of justifying it. Christian author Greg Koukl puts it like this, "Goodness is neither above God nor merely willed by Him. Instead, ethics are grounded in His holy character. Moral notions are not arbitrary and given to caprice. They are fixed and absolute, grounded in God's immutable nature." I've heard people say, "If your God is the standard of morality, then count me out!" Why? I believe it's because they have either misunderstood, misquoted, or have heard wrongly what they believe to be questionable events in the Bible. Author of *An Atheist's Values* Richard Robinson said in his book, "A god who was all-powerful but left much misery in the world would not be all-benevolent. An all-benevolent god in a world containing much misery would not be an all-powerful god. A world containing a god who was both all-powerful and all-benevolent would contain no misery."

So is God immoral for allowing evil to exist and to continue? Why doesn't He put a stop to all the evil acts that are constantly going on? If He is the standard of morality and He doesn't put a stop to all the evil, then wouldn't that prove He doesn't exist or that He's immoral? No, no, and no! Here's why. Atheist everywhere love to point out what they believe is a flaw for theism (usually Christianity), and that's the concern for all the evil that takes place on a daily basis (unless your Dawkins and don't believe in evil).

First, let us assume that God did get rid of all the evil in the world. To get rid of all the evil in the world, that means God would have to get rid of all humanity. Why? Because we all do evil, we all have sinned and fall short of the glory of God (Romans 3:23). None are righteous (Romans 3:10). So who would they like God to start with? Do they want God to start with themselves? With you? With me? My family? Your family? His/her family? It's funny when people mention God ridding the world of evil because they always want to point the finger at other people. Never do they point the finger at themselves.

What atheists fail to understand is even though it's logically possible for God to get rid of all the evil (which they won't like the results of that), it isn't actually achievable with a free will creation. Why?

There are some things God can't do. *What?* Yes, you read that correctly. Contrary to popular belief, there are a few things not even God can do. Before you close this book and write me off as a lunatic, let me explain. God can't create a being with free will and also force them to do only good. That's no longer free will. God can't create a married bachelor nor create a square circle. He can't give us free will and then force us not to commit evil. He also can't give us free will and force us to love. Love can't be forced by definition, but only given through free will. In fact, there are things we humans can do that God can't do. Do you know what that is? Sin. We can sin, but God cannot. C.S. Lewis said, "If a thing is free to be good, it is also free to be bad. And free will is what has made evil possible. Why then did God give them free will? Because free will, though it makes evil possible, it's also the only thing that makes possible any love or goodness or joy worth having." So by allowing us to freely love Him and do good things, it also gives us the right to not love Him and commit evil. Free will gives us all the right to choose between good and evil. If He takes away free will, He also takes away the good we have and love we have for Him and others.

God wanted a moral world, so, therefore, He created free will. If God was to stop people from committing evil, He's ultimately removing their free will (thus, not making this a moral world). God didn't create us to be robots and force us into loving Him. Forced love isn't love! A man can't force a woman to love Him. If He tries, she would only end up despising Him. Jon Morrison, a Christian author's rebuttal for this, says,

> Think about evil as you would think of counterfeit currency. A counterfeit is the corruption of something real. You can have real currency without the existence of any counterfeits. You cannot, however, have counterfeits without the real thing existing first. Evil is dependent on the existence of goodness but goodness is not dependent on evil. Goodness was there first. It is an absolute. Evil must always be thought of in relationship with absolute goodness.

I like to say that evil isn't an argument against God, but for God. How? We can have good without evil, but we can't have evil without good. It's like saying we can have the sun without shadows, but we can't have shadows without the sun. Shadows only prove the sun is shining. The same is with evil. Evil only confirms the presence of God's goodness. But once again, all this explanation of good and evil is unnecessary if atheists are using the words *good* and *evil* because without the standard of God's moral nature, they only have their subjective opinions to go on.

But what about diseases, hurricanes, tornadoes, earthquakes, and all the other worldly disasters? Doesn't that disprove God's existence? No! Why? Let's jump into an imaginary bubble for a minute and pretend cancers, and diseases, nor any earthly disasters ever existed. If we knew that our chances of living a much longer life was multiplied, then how careless would we be with our lives? We wouldn't be worried about much of anything because living a long life was almost inevitable. We most likely wouldn't bother to seek forgiveness until we were much older, and only then would we really start looking at the purpose of our own personal lives. And that probably wouldn't happen until we were well into our seventies and eighties. Not only that, but as mentioned before, we weren't designed to live forever in these bodies. Natural disasters, on the other hand, happen because the earth was never meant to be a permanent home for us. It's only temporary.

But everything that is considered evil on earth or bad is a result of our sin. Even the worldly disasters and diseases. How's that? After Adam had sinned, God tells Adam in Genesis 3:17–24, "Cursed is the ground for your sake." Basically, God cursed the earth because of our rebellion. A life with God (heaven) or a life without God (hell) is our eternal home, not earth. J. P. Moreland says, "God maintains a delicate balance between keeping His existence sufficiently evident so people will know He's there and yet hiding His presence enough so that people who want to choose to ignore Him can do it. This way, their choice of destiny is really free."

But God has many times gotten rid of evil. God did exactly what the atheist claim they want Him to do to prove Himself as the standard of good, and as God, and yet they still reject Him. When was this? Like in the day of Noah, "And God saw that the wickedness of man was great in the earth, and that every imagination of the thoughts of his heart was only evil continually" (Genesis 6:5). So God destroyed evil with a flood; but instead of atheist accepting Him, they now call Him evil and a moral monster for getting rid of evil. They also like to point out the time God had Israel destroy the Canaanites. Once again, God did exactly what atheists say He doesn't do, and He got rid of evil. Atheists can't make up their minds. Sorry, atheists, I meant brains.

I also want to point out that the majority of the atheist community is pro-choice, meaning, they are completely for abortion. Let me ask all my atheist readers this, "Why is it when God plays God, He's considered immoral. But when people play God, it's considered our moral right?" Let me know when anyone has an answer to that.

Back to what we were saying about the Canaanites. They were not good people. They were performing bestiality, sexual perversions, incest, murdering, and they were burning their babies alive in the molten hot arms of their god Moloch. The musicians would have to beat their drums extremely loud so the parents of the babies wouldn't have to hear their own babies screaming. So what did God do? God commanded the Israelites to destroy them. You mean all of them? No, not all of them. How do we know? The destroying of the Canaanites was a command of the Old Testament, and yet in the New Testament, one of Jesus's original twelve disciples Simon was a Canaanite (Matthew 10:4, Mark 3:18). But the Bible does say in Deuteronomy 20:17, "Completely destroy them—the Hittites, Amorites, Canaanites, Perizzites, Hivites, and Jebusites—as the Lord your God has commanded you." So if He wasn't commanding the Israelites to destroy all of them, why would the Bible say that? The entirety of the Bible isn't meant to be taken literally. Why? The Bible is written in many different styles (i.e., poetry, songs, wisdom, prophecy, apocalyptic, parables, history, metaphorical, hyperbole). Look at it this way. If I was to watch football and I said, "My team annihilated the other team!" would you think I meant that my team actually killed the other entire team? No, you would know I was speaking metaphorically. The same is with the Bible. So when people ask if I take the Bible literally, I tell them, "Where it's meant to be taken literally."

There's a great book by Paul Copan called *Is God a Moral Monster?* This book is great! I've read it more than once and is great for those trying to understand many questionable things of the Old Testament. He goes into much more details than I can here. The next biggest argument against God and His moral standards are all the atrocities throughout the Old Testament. Every time you turned around in the Old Testament, God was giving one command after another to the Israelites. Many of these commands seemed like nonsense at first glance, and other commands just seemed evil and cruel. Just a brief description of some of these are the following : You can't wear anything with mixed thread types. Don't eat pigs (I would've been a horrible candidate to live in those days. I love ham and bacon.) Don't boil a baby goat in its mother's milk. Don't eat fat (I and God agree on that one). Slavery seemed to have been endorsed. Many atheists also claim the Bible says if a woman's raped, she must marry the man who raped her. And the list goes on and on.

So why would God give such bizarre commands? First, I'd like to point out that these commands were not meant for everyone and for all times but specifically commanded for the Israelites in those days. Why? In the Old Testament days from the time of Adam to King Saul, Israel was in a theocracy. What's a theocracy? Theocracy is when people are governed by God, or those appointed by God. Another thing is a lot of those commands were given to separate God's holy people (the Israelites) from the rest of the world. He wanted His people to stand out among others and not to blend in. He wanted the rest of the world to know that the Israelites were His people and have different standards than the rest of them. Some of the commands were given to just keep the Israelites healthy, for instance, pigs. Pigs are filthy animals, delicious but filthy. In those days, they didn't have refrigerators or the technology we do now to properly clean and disinfect things. So by eating certain things could've possibly made them sick. A woman being forcibly raped and then forced to marry her rapist is just complete nonsense. The text they are quoting are taken out of context. Let's see what the Scripture actually says about rape in its entirety: "If a man meets a virgin who is not betrothed, and seizes her and lies with her, and they are found, then the man who lay with her shall give to the father of the young woman fifty shekels of silver, and she shall be his wife, because he has violated her. He may not divorce her all his days" (Deuteronomy 22:28–29). What this means in modern terms is if a man finds a girl and they have consensual sex and it's discovered, he has to marry her. For one, this kept people from sleeping around. Two, it stopped men from sleeping around and then dumping women, and three, this also gave women in those days financial security.

Let's look at the next verse,

> But if in the open country a man meets a young woman who is betrothed, and the man seizes her and lies with her, then only the man who lay with her shall die. But you shall do nothing to the young woman; she has committed no offense punishable by death. For this case is like that of a man attacking and murdering his neighbor, because he met her in the open country, and though the betrothed young woman cried for help there was no one to rescue her. (Deuteronomy 22:25–27)

What's the difference between the two commands? In these last two verses, it clearly states that the woman cried out. She was not a willing participant, and this was not consensual. She was raped. This makes it clear where the Bible stands on rape. The rapists were to be put to death. What about slavery? In the Old Testament, it does speak of slavery. But hold your horses. We first must understand slavery in biblical times. Slavery back in biblical days was not the same as the slavery term we think of today. Slavery wasn't race based. It was servitude. People who owed others money but could not pay up would voluntarily work for the owners of fields to pay off their debt. (Leviticus 25:39). The masters were not allowed to beat, kill, neglect, nor keep the servant forever (Exodus 21:20–27,

Exodus 21:2, Deuteronomy 15:12). No matter the cost owed, six years was the maximum amount of work the masters could get from their servants. Servitude was also a way people made money to take care of their families. It was much like an employer-employee-type relationship. If masters (basically employers) caused harm to their servants (employees), they would have to pay (Exodus 21:20–27). Sometimes even after the debt was paid, many servants would stay with their masters because they had become like one of the family (Exodus 20:5–6; Deuteronomy 15:16–17).

There were some people from outside the Israelites that wanted to join with the Israelites, and they would be forced to do work. The master had to abide by the same rules though, as if the person was an Israelite, no beating, no hitting, no killing, no mistreatment, and so forth (Exodus 12:44). After wars, when the Israelites would take people captive, they were forced to work as well, but it was so they wouldn't rally up and try to overthrow the Israelites. But once again, the same rules applied except the gaining of their freedom after six years (Deuteronomy 20:14, Leviticus 25:44–46). As you can see through the many examples given, *slavery* (the word used in the twenty-first-century sense) nor rape were condoned. Once again, the book *Is God a Moral Monster?* covers all these questions, concerns, and confusions in much more detail.

Without a universal moral standard from God, then only moral relativism applies. What's moral relativism? Simply put, whatever culture you grow up in, that's your moral compass. If your culture says it's okay to burn alive the second-born child, then it's okay. If your culture says it's normal to rape women, then that's okay. Nothing is objective. Look back at our example earlier on if the Nazis would've succeeded by taking over the world, a scary thought actually. So does this "evidence" point to God being a moral monster? Or does it show that the ones reading the Bible aren't interpreting the Bible correctly? Does the evidence point to morality being an act of evolution? Or does the evidence for morality point to a moral law giver we call God? I'll let you decide.

A RIPPLE IN TIME

Have you ever heard of the ripple effect? Have you ever had something happen in your life, and you don't understand the cause of it but later on you see the benefits from it? Sometimes when God does things, we don't know the cause of it until later on because He uses what's known as the ripple effect. Other times, we may never know the cause because His ways are higher than our ways. His thoughts are higher than our thoughts. But everything we do has a ripple effect.

Have you ever witnessed the ripple effect? What is the ripple effect? The ripple effect is when something is done at one point in time; and later on, sometimes thousands of years later, we see the effect of that action. God uses the ripple effect to get His desired results. Don't believe this can happen? Just ask Marty Mcfly from *Back to the Future*. He messed with the space-time continuum, and the ripple effects from that were catastrophic. That's until he was able to right the wrongs before the end of the movie. We can sometimes see the ripple effect throughout our lives. For example, when a husband and wife decide to have kids, they lay with one another; and nine months later, a baby is born. That's the ripple effect. We also see the ripple effect throughout the Bible.

The most notorious ripple effect is the story of Joseph (Genesis 37–50). Joseph was sold into slavery by his own brothers. After years of being a slave and a prisoner, Joseph ends up becoming the second in command to Pharaoh. Due to Joseph being in God's favor, he rose to power and saved many people from the seven-year famine that struck Egypt, including his own brothers who sold him into slavery.

Joseph told his brothers, "You planned evil against me; God planned it for good to bring about the present result—the survival of many people" (Genesis 50:20). From the time Joseph was sold into slavery to the time of the famine in Egypt was approximately twenty to twenty-five years. We never know what kind of outcome the ripple effect will have throughout the course of history.

Country singer Randy Travis had a number one hit song called "Three Wooden Crosses" that showed the ripple effect. To summarize the song, four people were on a bus: a teacher, preacher, farmer, and a prostitute. The bus has an accident, and three of them were killed except the prostitute. As the preacher was dying, he gave his Bible to the prostitute; and years later, she had a son who ends up becoming a preacher. And he's the one telling the story in the song.

But not all ripple effects are for God's intended purpose. When someone commits a crime and years later they're caught for it and go to prison is an example of a ripple effect that wasn't caused by God. The point of a godly ripple effect is for God to get His desired outcome. We never know the purpose God has for all the things He does and all the things He allows to happen, including the things we find to be wrong or evil. We don't know His thoughts. We don't understand His logic (Isaiah 55:8). God has a purpose for everything He allows on earth. He knows the beginning to the end before the universe was created. He's outside the realm of time, so everything that's happening for us now He's already seen it. He can see the ripple effect of every one of our actions.

Indulge me for a moment. There's a car crash. All occupants live except a two-year-old boy named Daniel. Paramedics get on the scene. The paramedic, trying his hardest to resuscitate the baby, is an atheist. Years later, the parents of that child still struggle with why that had to happen to their child. What they don't see is years later, that atheist paramedic who worked on their baby felt such sadness and sorrow for not being able to save that little boy quits his job the next day and went to work odd jobs while he drank his depression away. At one of his jobs was a coworker who was a Christian man. Over time and through many talks about the power of forgiveness through Jesus Christ, this once-promising paramedic turned drunk, depressed, atheist man gives his life over to God. He goes on to marry a Christian woman, with whom he had a son and named him Daniel. Daniel goes on to become a preacher at a local church, helping to lead thousands to Christ. Out of those thousands who are brought to Christ, hundreds go on to become evangelicals, preachers, apologists, missionary workers, and the ripple effect continues for decades, and even to centuries.

As the parents of the deceased child get older, they lose their faith in God over what happened to their child. Now here, they are in their late eighties, and they see a Christian pastor from Africa telling the story of how he was saved, and it all rippled back to a car accident many years ago and with the loss of one little boy named Daniel. The parents, now seeing the ripple effect, turn back to God. Maybe I should've been a fiction writer. Now this is just a story, but it outlines how the ripple effect can happen even out of tragedy.

I've told this story many times, and a few times I've had people ask me, "So God allowed an innocent child to die and other families to suffer, just so there would be a ripple effect?" Hmm, did I mention the story was made up? No child was actually harmed in this illustration. But assuming it was true, like I said before, God lives outside the realm of time. He sees the beginning to the end. God is just. God knew that baby would be back in heaven with Him. He also knew the parents would see the ripple effect and understand what happened had a reason and would turn back to Him. This doesn't mean you have to agree with God's reason, but you have no other choice but to accept it.

Before we were born, God set the times and places where we would live. He knows where we will be born and live, when we will be born, and when we will die. He created us for His purpose. Who are we to say what He can do with His creation? It would be the same as if Michelangelo had torn up the Sistine Chapel after he was done painting it. You can't be mad at him for destroying his own masterpiece. Same is with God. We might not understand it. We don't have to like it, but we can't call God evil for doing what He does with His own creation. Does that make God immoral? No, because He's the giver and taker of life. We are His creation. How do we have free will then if God has already determined when we are born, where we will live, and when we will die? If you're an atheist, the answer's simple. We don't have free will. We're just colliding molecules dancing to the music of our own DNA. You're just following the predestination of the evolutionary effect of your brain. Remember, according to atheists, our brains are the product of molecules clashing and reacting together. For everyone else, some might say, "If all this is determined before I'm born, then I'm not acting on free will, only reacting in accordance to God's predetermination for my life. If that is true, then anything I do, whether it be good or evil, was predestined by God, right?" No. Why? Look at it like this. You watch sports, and your team was playing tonight, but you had prior engagements. You decide to record the game on your DVR and just figured you would watch the game after you were done. Later on that night, you're driving home and are all excited to watch the game. Your buddy calls you on your way to the house and says, "I can't believe we won 26 to 7." Aww, man! You didn't want to know the score! You wanted to watch the game. Regardless of knowing the score you decide to watch the game anyways because you want to see how it all plays out. If you are watching the recorded game hours after it had already been played, does that mean the guys on your TV didn't have free will? You already know the outcome, the game's already been won, so by you already knowing the outcome doesn't take away their free will. The same is with God. He's outside the realm of time. He's already seen how the game of "life" is going to play out. He already knows the final score. We have free will, even though God knows the end results. If God knows the end results before the universe was even created, is He not able to see from the beginning to the end and determine how far the ripple effects will go? Yes! If He is all-powerful and all-knowing and cannot interfere with free will without taking away our free will, then isn't He able to use His creation any way He chooses to get the results He's wanting? Of course! We might not understand some of the things that happen in our lives. We might not be able to see the good in all tragedies, and we might not ever see the outcome of all the ripple effects. The shortest answer to this might not be the most comforting nor the most satisfying, but we are going to just have to put our trust in the one who does know the outcome and the purpose behind it.

JML Monsabré who lived during the 1800s puts it best, "If God would concede me His power (omnipotence) for 24 hours, you would see how many changes I would make in the world. But if He gave me His wisdom too, I would leave things as they are." Having the power of God would be useless without having His wisdom as well. In the movie *Bruce Almighty* starring Jim Carrey, Jennifer Aniston, and Morgan Freeman, we can see what happens when Bruce (Jim Carrey) is endowed with God's (Morgan Freeman) powers for seven days just within the city of Buffalo, New York. Bruce begins his adventure by righting all the wrongs in his own personal life and proceeds to grant everyone else's prayers to them. Everyone was winning the lottery, sports teams were winning who had never won before. Bruce got the promotion he wanted from work, and he thought life couldn't get any better. But then things took a turn for the worse, and by the end of the seven days, his life was a mess. His fiancée (Jennifer Aniston) had left him, the entire town was in an uproar, and everything was out of control. Now, of course, by the end of the movie, God put everything back in order.

I know this was a movie, but it's actually a very good representation of two things, one being that the power of God would not be good without the wisdom of God. Two, it showed us the ripple effect. When everyone in the movie got what they wanted when they asked for it, the entire city was almost in ruins by the end of the seven days. In this movie, it shows through the ripple effect why God says yes to some prayers and no to others. God is our heavenly parent. Just like on earth, when we raise our children, sometimes our answers to them are no; and to them, it seems as if we're being mean and cruel. The answer isn't no because we don't love them. It's no because we do love them, and we can see the outcome of what the ripple effect is going to be. With all of us being sinners and God being sin-free and perfect, how much more loving is He going to be and do what is best for all of us?

WHY CHRISTIANITY?

Out of all the gods people claim, and with all the religions in the world, which god is the one true God? How do we know Yahweh, the Christian God, is the one true God? What evidence do we have to support such a claim, and what about all the other religions? Did you know that there are over four thousand different religions worldwide? Although some of these religions share some similarities, there are huge major differences that separate them, and only one can be true. Why's that? Because if only one of them is true, then all the others have to be false. If not, it would be breaking the laws of logic (the law of excluded middle to be exact). That law basically states, in layman's terms, something can't be true and false at the same time. The majority of these religions can be classified into separate categories. They are either polytheism, which is the belief in many gods (e.g., sun God, water God, air God, and so forth), monotheism which is the belief in only one God—monotheism is also known as having a theistic god—which means having only one god (e.g., Judaism, Christianity, Islam, etc.), animism which is the belief that plants, trees, and so on are a form of a god, pantheism which believes all is god (such as the universe and all that's in it), totemism believes that humans and other natural beings have a divine connection (a person also has its animal spirit), and atheism (no god at all).

I just want to take a brief moment to dissect why we can rule out a lot of these categories of religions as having the true God. First, we need to identify what we mean when we say *god*. God is an all-knowing, all-powerful, personal, timeless, spaceless, immaterial, eternal, infinite, moral, perfect being. So right out the door, we can exclude any religion categorized in pantheism (the belief in many gods). Why's that? Multiple reasons, there can't be more than one all-powerful, all-knowing God. Now why's that? Because if there are two gods, then that means one is lacking what the other has. If one is lacking, then it isn't perfect nor all-powerful, meaning, it can't be God.

Another reason is God must be eternal and infinite (having no beginning and no ending). We know for certainty the sun and the stars and the moon and so forth had a beginning; and we also know that stars, such as our own sun, is running out of energy and will someday collapse on itself and be no more. Anything that has a beginning can't be eternal or infinite. And the last reason, though I'm sure there's many more, is the sun and moon and all the other gods in pantheism aren't all-powerful or personal or timeless or spaceless or immaterial. How come? Because they're created in space, out of material, and within time since it has a beginning. They can't be all-powerful if the sun is slowly dying.

Next on the list is animism. This is the belief that plants, trees, and so on are all gods. This category is a fallacy in many areas. How come? Plants, trees, and anything else is the result of either a creation from an external force, or they're created by necessity out of nature (also known as the contingency argument). If it's created by an external force, then that external force would have a better chance of being a god than the creation itself; and if it's created by necessity out of nature, then it doesn't explain how the universe got here to begin with because the universe couldn't have been created out of necessity by nature before nature had a beginning. Did I say that right? Also, just as with pantheism, there can't be more than one god without one or the other lacking in something. That's a mouthful and a lot to let sink in. If you got that, then let's keep moving forward.

Next on the list is totemism (believing people and animals are divinely connected). If humans are in any form or fashion divine, then we have a huge problem. Why's that? Because everyone knows humans aren't eternal or infinite, whether you choose to believe we are the product of macroevolution (goo to you via the zoo) or were created by some other means. The origins of humanity have a beginning. Nor are we all-powerful, all knowing, timeless, spaceless, and/or immaterial. The same goes with any animal on the planet as well.

Second to the last we have atheism. Atheism used to be classified as a person who lacks a belief in anything relating to a God. The reason I included it in a category of religions is because in the last twenty to thirty years, atheism has become more of a form of religion. How's that? Mainly it's due to atheist wanting to push atheism on to people and because even though they claim it's a lack of belief, it's still a belief. If they don't believe in a god, that's still a form of belief. If they believe there is no God, they are exerting a belief. So therefore, they are a form of religion. Atheism fails if you believe that the universe and all that is in it have a design and a creator. If you choose to believe that everything existing today is by luck or chance, then you would be considered an atheist. No one created something from nothing is the most dominant atheistic view of the universe and the world.

Lastly, we need to examine monotheism or the possibility of a theistic god (meaning, only one God). Well, having only one God is a good start and already sets it above all the other categories already discussed. Why's that? Having only one God can already pass the laws of logic. It eliminates any other need for any other being and/or necessity creation and can be seen as an all knowing, all-powerful, personal, timeless, spaceless, immaterial, eternal, infinite, perfect being that the characteristics of a God needs in order for the universe to have been created and all that's in it.

All right, so to sum it up, we have eliminated all religious categories down to one, and we've gotten rid of approximately 98 percent of all religions. So which religions are categorized as monotheism or theism? The three largest and most well-known religions are Judaism, Islam, and Christianity. Let us now explore all three religions individually and see which one leads to the most probable, logical one true God.

The first religion we'll look at is Judaism. In a nutshell, Judaism is half of Christianity. What do I mean? Judaism is the Old Testament of the Christian Bible. Jews refer to their Bible as the Tanakh. Judaism and Christianity believe in the same god, "Yahweh." Where the two are completely opposite is the New Testament and the believing in Jesus of Nazareth as the Messiah. Jews don't believe the New Testament is God-inspired or that Jesus of Nazareth is the Messiah. They are still waiting on Him. How come they don't believe in Jesus as the Messiah? They believe a redeemed world would have no violence, no hunger, world peace, and all this will be due to a worldly king sitting on his throne, making it all happen.

I do believe in the Hebrew original Scripture, but not all the Jewish bible known as the Tanakh. What do I mean? A thousand years before Jesus was born, the original Hebrew Scripture was written in ancient Hebrew. As time went on, many people no longer could speak, write, or read ancient Hebrew. Most of the common world language was Greek. The king of Greece at the time was King Ptolemy, Philadelphus. He wanted to know the God of Israel but couldn't speak or read ancient Hebrew. He sent for seventy-two Jewish rabbis (six from each tribe of Israel) to come to him and translate the Hebrew text into Greek so he and others could understand it. This translation came to be known as the Septuagint.

Septuagint is the Latin word for seventy, representing the seventy-two rabbis who translated it. The Septuagint was accepted by the Sanhedrin of that time who, in comparison, is basically like what the Vatican is to the Catholics today. The Septuagint ended up having around sixty-six total books. The Christian Bible uses the Septuagint text in their Bible, but not all their books. Why? It is the closest thing we have to the original Hebrew Scriptures, but we disagree on the validation of all sixty-six books.

Here's why. Over a thousand years later and after the death and resurrection of Jesus Christ, around AD 70, the second temple in Jerusalem was destroyed, resulting in the loss of most of the original Hebrew Scriptures. A group of Jewish rabbis known as the Masoretes decided to retranslate the original Hebrew Scriptures in fear of losing the Word of God entirely. Unfortunately, they did not have the original Scriptures in hand, so they translated the Scripture by oral translation. What's oral translation? Oral translation was very common in those days and relied on memory skills. Jewish rabbis were taught to remember all the Old Testament Bible by memory.

These texts came to be known as the Masoretic text. The Masoretic text contains the thirty-nine books we Christians now use in our Old Testament. So Christians use the Septuagint text, but the Masoretic number of books for their Bible, while Judaism uses both the text and number of books from the Masoretic text. The Bible now used by Judaism is what is known as the Tanakh.

There are over one hundred predictions in the Old Testament that point to Jesus of Nazareth as the Messiah. There are two prophecies that are irrefutable. For example, Isaiah 7:14 says, "Therefore the Lord Himself will give you a sign: The virgin will conceive and give birth to a son, and will call him Immanuel." Another is Psalm 22:16, "For dogs surround me; they have pierced my hands and feet."

After reading just those two scriptures, how is it then that Jews don't believe in Jesus as the prophesied Messiah? Well, when the Masoretes created the Masoretic text by oral translation which is now the Tanakh, their verses say slightly different things. For example, in the Tanakh, Isaiah 7:14 says, "Assuredly, my Lord will give you a sign of His own accord! Look, the *young woman* is with child and about to give birth to a son. Let her name him Immanuel." And again, in Psalms 22:16, which in the Tanakh is verse 17, says, "Dogs surround me; a pack of evil ones closes in on me, like lions they *maul* my hands and feet." Notice the Christian Bible says the woman was a virgin in Isaiah, and in the Tanakh, it refers to her just as a young woman. And in Psalms of the Christian Bible, it says He was pierced; but once again, in the Tanakh, it says He was mauled.

There are several assumptions as to why these translations defer. One reason is rabbis who performed the oral translation into the Masoretic text didn't recognize Jesus as the Messiah, so they purposely changed the words so it wouldn't lead to Jesus. And since at this time the Sanhedrin was no more, they had no authority to answer to. Another possible assumption is it was just an honest mistake. Nobody really knows. So the Christian Bible uses the Septuagint text with the Masoretic number of books, and the Tanakh uses the Masoretic text and the Masoretic number of books.

I personally tend to believe that the Septuagint is a more accurate translation from the original Scripture. Why? A couple of different reasons actually. It was written over one thousand years before Jesus was born, and Jesus fulfilled the prophecies. It was copied from seventy-two rabbis, six from each tribe of the twelve tribes of Israel, and was approved by the Sanhedrin. Finally, it was actually copied from the original ancient Hebrew Scriptures and not just memorized over a thousand years and then orally translated.

Stoner, Chairman of the Departments of Mathematics and Astronomy at Pasadena College, formulated the odds of all the Old Testament predictions with all of them coming true in Jesus of Nazareth, and those odds are 1 in 10 to the 17th power! So with the Old Testament pointing to Christ and Him fulfilling all those predictions and all the eyewitness testimonies, plus philosophical evidence, it's hard not to believe that Jesus is the Messiah spoken about in the Old Testament. Testimonies of Jesus of Nazareth are the exact same as the coming Messiah of the Old Testament. Jesus Himself, being a Jew, had no reason to lie about who He was and why He was here. He gained nothing by saying He was God/the Son of God. Jesus, being a Jew, would've thought of Himself as a blasphemer for making such claims if they weren't true. Here are some other Old Testament verses that spoke of the coming Messiah:

> Seventy weeks are determined upon thy people and upon thy holy city, to finish the transgression, and to make an end of sins, and to make reconciliation for iniquity, and to bring in everlasting righteousness, and to seal up the vision and prophecy, and to anoint the most Holy. Know therefore and understand, that from the going forth of the commandment to restore and to build Jerusalem unto the Messiah the Prince shall be seven weeks, and threescore and two weeks: the street shall be built again, and the wall, even in troublous times. And after threescore and two weeks shall Messiah be cut off, but not for himself: and the people of the prince that shall come shall destroy the city and the sanctuary; and the

end thereof shall be with a flood, and unto the end of the war desolations are determined. And he shall confirm the covenant with many for one week: and in the midst of the week he shall cause the sacrifice and the oblation to cease, and for the overspreading of abominations he shall make it desolate, even until the consummation, and that determined shall be poured upon the desolate. (Daniel 9:24–27)

The Lord will raise up for you a prophet like me from among yourselves, from your own kinsmen. You are to pay attention to him … I will raise up for them a prophet like you from among their kinsmen. I will put my words in his mouth, and he will tell them everything I order him. (Deuteronomy 18:15)

And David my servant [shall be] king over them; and they all shall have one shepherd: they shall also walk in my judgments, and observe my statutes, and do them. (Ezekiel 37:24–27)

When Israel was a child, I loved him, and out of Egypt I called my son. (Hosea 1:1)

And he shall be for a sanctuary; but for a stone of stumbling and for a rock of offense to both the houses of Israel, for a gin and for a snare to the inhabitants of Jerusalem. (Isaiah 8:14)

Nevertheless, there will be no more gloom for those who were in distress. In the past he humbled the land of Zebulun and the land of Naphtali, but in the future he will honor Galilee of the nations, by the Way of the Sea, beyond the Jordan. (Isaiah 8:23–9:1)

For a child has been born to us, a son given to us, and the authority is upon his shoulder, and the wondrous adviser, the mighty God, the everlasting Father, called his name, 'the prince of peace.'" (Isaiah 9:6–7)

And he shall set up a banner for the nations, and shall assemble the outcasts of Israel, and gather together the dispersed of Judah from the four corners of the earth. (Isaiah 11:12)

Therefore thus saith the Lord God, Behold, I lay in Zion for a foundation a stone, a tried stone, a precious corner stone, a sure foundation: he that believeth shall not make haste. (Isaiah 28:16)

But he was wounded for our transgressions, he was bruised for our iniquities: the chastisement of our peace was upon him, and with his stripes we are healed. (Isaiah 53:5)

Then was fulfilled that which was spoken by Jeremiah the prophet, saying, "In Rama was there a voice heard, lamentation, and weeping, and great mourning, Rachel weeping for her children, and would not be comforted, because they are not." (Jeremiah 31:15–18)

But thou, Beth-lehem Ephrathah, which art little to be among the thousands of Judah, out of thee shall one come forth unto Me that is to be ruler in Israel; whose goings forth are from of old, from ancient days. (Micah 5:2)

The list goes on: Psalms 2, 16, 22, 34, 69, 110; 2 Samuel 7:14; Zechariah 9:9; Zechariah 12:10; and a few more. All these point to a coming Messiah. Jesus of Nazareth fits every single one of these descriptions. The only logical conclusion, or at the very least a high probability, is that Jesus is the Messiah that was told would come in the Old Testament.

The next religion for us to discuss is Islam. Does Islam follow the Jewish and Christian god Yahweh? Absolutely not. Allah is the god they follow. The biggest difference between Christianity and Islam is Christians believe they have a Savior (Jesus Christ) in which our sins are forgiven. Islam doesn't believe in a savior but believe that through their works, they will be judged and deemed good enough to make it into heaven. If God is the standard of justice, then how do Muslims propose that God will remove their sins if nobody has paid the penalty? They believe their good works will get them a "free pass" into heaven. That kind of logic doesn't even work here on earth! What do I mean? Imagine I go off and commit all kinds of crimes. I get speeding tickets, I steal, I murder, and do many more crimes. Finally, I have to stand before the judge to be judged for my crimes. The judge asks me "What do you have to say for yourself?" I begin naming all the charities I give to, all the poor I have helped, all the homeless I have sheltered, the hungry I have fed, all the places I have volunteered. After I'm done telling the judge all the good I have done, do you think the judge will let me go? Would we expect the judge to take all my good deeds and wipe away all my bad? Or do we expect the judge to say, "Well, thank you for all you've done, but I'm not here to judge you on the things you've done good. I'm here to judge you on what you have done wrong."

If we hadn't done anything wrong, then there would be no need to judge us. Judges don't sit around waiting to tell people good job on all the things we've gotten right. Judges are here to place disciplinary actions on the things we have done wrong. God is the standard of that justice! He's going to tell us good job for the things we've done right, but He's also going to discipline us for all the sins (crimes) we've committed. It's only through Jesus Christ can the judgment of our sins not come back on us. If Islam doesn't believe that someone has paid the penalty for our sins, then that means when we die, we will have to face the wrath of God for all our sins. Jesus has taken that wrath for us. It isn't through works we gain Jesus's gift of salvation (Ephesians 2:9). It is a gift.

Islam also worships Muhammad. Muhammad was a man born in Arabia in AD 570 and died in AD 632. He claimed to be a messenger of God, who received revelation. This revelation came to him at the age of forty by Gabriel the angel (so he claims). He started preaching about his revelations approximately in AD 613. Muhammad himself claims in the Quran that he never performed miracles of any kind. That in itself strikes me as odd because all of God's prophets, who were revealing new revelation from God performed miracles to confirm that the revelation was indeed from God, except Muhammad. Islam does recognize Jesus but only as a prophet who died but never rose again. If Jesus never rose, then death was never defeated, and Jesus wasn't the Son of God. So if Islam is correct and Christianity is false, then we are all in a lot of trouble on judgment day. In fact, just recently Frank Turek points out how if the Quran (the Islam bible) is true, it's still false. Now how's that? By looking at the book Surah in Quran chapter 5 verse 68, it says this, "O People of the Book [speaking of Jews and Christians]! You have nothing to stand on unless you observe the Torah, the Gospel, and what has been revealed to you from your Lord." So what the Quran is saying is we all need to listen to the Old Testament, the gospels, and the revelation given to the other authors of the New Testament. That's exactly what Christians do. Their prophet Mohammad testified to many new revelations, but they aren't trustworthy since Mohammad, by his own omission, never performed miracles to back up his revelation. If his revelation isn't true, then following what the Quran says in Surah points you to Christianity. That's a tongue twister. By processes of elimination, either the Quran isn't true, or it is, and it points us to Christianity.

And now lastly, Christianity. What is Christianity's beliefs? Christianity is the belief in one God (Yahweh) and in Jesus of Nazareth being God/the son of God in human flesh, living a perfect life, dying on the cross for all our sins, and then rising back to life three days later, and it's only through belief in Him we have salvation and eternal life in heaven.

So how can we know the stories of Jesus of Nazareth are true? Let's look into the evidence and proof of Jesus being who He says He was and the evidence that He died and rose again. First, we must look at who the Bible claims Jesus is. "The Father and I are one" (John 10:30). "You must have the same attitude that Christ Jesus had. Though He was God, He did not think of equality with God as something to cling to" (Philippians 2:5–6). "As the Father is in me, and I in Him, they also maybe one in Us" (John 1:18). "No one has seen God, but the one and only Son, who is Himself God" (John 17:21). "In the beginning was the Word, and the Word was with God, and the Word was God" (John 1:1). "And the Word became flesh and dwelt among us" (John 1:14).

The Bible seems to make it clear in many places that Jesus is God/the Son of God. But still, how do we know that it's true? Well, just like any mystery, we have to look into the eyewitness's testimony. Let's start with the four gospels: Matthew, Mark, Luke, and John. The first question that comes to mind is, couldn't the writers of the gospels been lying? Yes, but that wouldn't be logical. Why? Because all the gospel writers were already Jews except for Luke (Luke was a doctor). Jews already had the Torah (the first five books of the Bible) and believed they were already saved without Jesus. Why would they give eyewitness details about the life and death of Jesus if they already believed they were saved? What Jesus claimed was considered blasphemy according to the Jews. Matthew, Mark, and John were going against everything they believed in and had been taught from birth. But why would they do that? It's because they believed in Jesus being God/the son of God so much that they were all willing to and did die for their belief in Him. One might say, "People lie all the time. People write books and give interviews in which they know they are lying. What makes them any different?" That's true, but people know when they are lying. And nobody who's lying is willing to die for a lie in which they know they're lying about. Did I say that right? Also, we have to keep in mind that all four gospels were written at different times and in different locations. The book of Mark was written in either Rome or Jerusalem around AD 66–70. Matthew was either written in Syrian Antioch or Jerusalem AD 85–90. Luke, according to scholars, was written in Antioch or Asia Minor AD 85–90, and John written in Ephesus AD 90–110. It's not as if these men were all sitting around a campfire and discussing what to say and what not to say. It wasn't like, "Hey Mark! How about we say that Jesus called Peter Satan? What do you think of that?" Can you see how ridiculous that actually sounds? "Okay, but all the books were written years after when they had claimed the actual events of Jesus occurred." That's true, but so were all history books, and we still believe them to be true.

Why should the account of the New Testament gospels be considered less than any other history book? All four books claim the life of Jesus was anything less than extraordinary. They all speak of His miracles, His life, His death, and His resurrection. After the resurrection of Jesus, over five hundred people witnessed seeing Him (1 Corinthians 15:3–8). Even in the United States court system, it takes only two eyewitnesses to convict someone to prison. We're completely okay with the eyewitness account of only two people to convict someone to prison for life, and yet we struggle to believe the eyewitness' testimony of over five hundred people? Why is that? It turns out that many people see the eyewitness accounts of Jesus's resurrection as unreliable due to how long ago it happened, and they never personally saw Jesus and all He had done. But if that's the logic we're going to use here, then I guess we can't say for absolute certainty that Abraham Lincoln, George Washington, or John Adams ever lived. Why? Because nobody today saw, met, or knew any of these men. All we have to go on are history books and their legacy, and we accept all of them as true and accurate.

Paul of Tarsus, who was previously known as Saul, wrote many accounts of Jesus. (Over one-half of the New Testament writings are accredited to Paul). Paul was a Jew just like the other three gospel writers. Paul was actually one of the most feared Jewish men by the Christian community of that time. Why? He was a Roman soldier who was in charge of killing and imprisoning all those that were followers of Jesus. He was a murderer of Christians! He actually stood there and gave approval of the first known martyr Stephen. Paul thought what he was doing by killing all the Christians was the work of God. Paul had no reason to make up a story about his conversion. In his eyes, he was already saved. If anything, he probably figured he would be at the right hand of God. He didn't think he needed Jesus to be saved. But then Jesus came to Paul on the road to Damascus, and after that, Paul believed in Him. After his conversion, Paul went on to become one of the most prolific authors of the New Testament. He is attributed to writing somewhere between thirteen to fourteen books out of the twenty-seven books of the New Testament.

So why would Paul, a Jewish soldier and hater of Jesus and Christianity, makes claims against his own beliefs, spend most of the rest of his life in prisons and ultimately die because of his assurance in Jesus as Lord of Lords? Wouldn't it make more sense that he and the others would've recanted their claims before being killed for their beliefs in Jesus if they were false? What did they have to gain? Nothing! Why? When they wrote the gospels, and when Paul wrote his books, they never gained success, money, power, popularity, or fame. Just the exact opposite actually happened. They were repeatedly thrown into prisons, beaten, and eventually murdered for their beliefs. For someone to have gone through all that after already believing they were saved without Jesus could only mean one thing; and that would be what they witnessed, what they had seen, and what they believed was the absolute truth. Doesn't the Old Testament and New Testament have contradictions? Yes, they do. Doesn't contradictions prove it's fallacy? No. Why? What many see as contradictions are actually just known errors. "Are you saying the Bible has errors?" Yes. Why? We can see the few errors in the Bible by comparing the many manuscripts to one other. In virtually almost all cases of known errors, scribes were able to recognize these errors and correct them. "Doesn't the Bible having errors prove it can't be true?" No. The Bible having errors doesn't prevent us from knowing what the main topic being expressed was. Here's an example of what I mean. Let us pretend that we found three manuscripts of John chapter 10 verse 30.

Manuscript 1: "I and the Fath#r are one."
Manuscript 2: "I and the Fat#er are one."

Manuscript 3: "I and the Fa#her are one."

Now by looking at these three manuscripts, are we able to conclude what the Bible was saying? Yes, of course, we can. The total number of actual Greek manuscripts of the New Testament stacked over a mile high. That's huge considering most Greek classical literature manuscripts barely made it to four feet high. People have asked, "Why wouldn't God have just preserved the original?" That's a great question. Let's assume God did preserve the original manuscript. What could we do with that original copy? We could alter it, change it, and/or destroy it all together; and nobody would know the difference. Why's that? Because we would have nothing to compare the altered or changed manuscripts to. What God did do was have over four hundred copies of the original made and passed out to different people. Why would He do that? If someone would have changed any one of their copies, we would know who changed their copy and call them out on it. If all 399 manuscripts say one thing, but only one was different, then we know who changed theirs, and we know where the change was made, making it easy to correct. Simply put, by not preserving the original He preserved, the original.

But what if the errors aren't as subtle as the example I gave? What about the gospel's account of the resurrection of Jesus? Some say one angel was present at the tomb, another two angels, and others differ on who showed up to the tomb first. So which gospel account is correct? I believe all of them are correct. How's that? Every book was written from that person's own personal experiences and viewpoints. Let's say four people see a crime, and the police show up to take down their eyewitness reports separately. What you will hear are four different stories of how the crime happened. One witness saw only one male suspect. Another witness saw two male suspects. Another witness noticed one male and one female, and the fourth witness only saw one female. Are any of them lying? No. They all saw things from different perspectives, but through their testimony as a whole, police are able to combine them together and get an accurate account of how the crime happened. It is because of these types of errors, I believe, give validation to the stories and accounts of Jesus of Nazareth. Think about it. If every witness gave the exact same descriptions and details of what happened, it would look as if they had gotten together and collaborated the entire story, and none of their testimonies would be valid.

Let's use a true, more famous example, one of the most tragic events to ever occur in modern US history, the 9/11 attacks in New York City. Some of the eyewitness accounts say that an explosion occurred before either of the planes hit the world trade centers. Other witnesses say it was a commercial plane while others claim it didn't look like a commercial plane at all. Does having several different contradicting eyewitness testimonies mean we can't put together what happened during the 9/11 attacks? Of course not! We know the main point of the event. The same applies to the stories of Jesus, including His resurrection. Though the testimonies have slight variations, the main objective was to express that Jesus is God/the Son of God. He died on the cross and rose again in three days.

American scholar and great skeptic Bart Ehrman wrote a book in 2005 titled *Misquoting Jesus*. His stance was that the New Testament documents could not be historically proven to be accurate, so therefore, they are not accurate and unreliable. Within a year or two, a paperback version of the same book comes out; and on page 252, he says, "Christian beliefs are not affected by textual variants in the manuscript tradition of the New Testament." He openly admits that the New Testament variants are not even enough to affect Christianity. The testimonies from the New Testament writers were also extremely embarrassing. How? Well, in many places where the Bible speaks about the original twelve disciples was in an embarrassing manor. Where? John 12:16, Mark 9:32, and in Luke 18:34 all show how dingy the disciples were. Jesus says something to them or in front of them, and when away from everyone else, they have to ask Jesus what He meant by that. They didn't understand many of His parables.

In Luke 26:33, Peter tries acting like a big shot, with his chest puffed out in front of the other disciples and tells Jesus, "Even if everyone else falls away, I never will. I'll follow you to death." But then what happens? He cowards down and denies Jesus three separate times when asked by the people if he knew Jesus. In Mark 8:33, Jesus calls Peter Satan in front of everyone. Can you imagine? Peter being the rock of Christianity and somewhat of a leader to the other eleven disciples was called Satan in front of all his friends. I mean, here's Peter, thinking he was high and mighty and of great importance; and then Jesus, the Messiah, the Son of God, their teacher referred to him as God's greatest enemy! How embarrassing would that be?

There's even embarrassing testimony about Jesus as well. Like what, you might ask. Jesus had to be placed in a borrowed tomb! Think about it. Jesus, the Son of God, and they are having to borrow a tomb to place His body in (Luke 23:50–56). His disciples who were with Him the majority of His three years of preaching and teaching didn't even bother to try to give Him a proper burial! And then in John 7:5, it tells us that even Jesus's own brothers didn't believe He was the Messiah. This was Jesus's own flesh and blood. These people grew up with Him and knew Him best and not even they believed He was the Christ!

In the same book of John, in verse, 20 they tell us how crowds thought Jesus was demon possessed. Imagine this. Here we have the disciples who abandoned their own religion of Judaism, now claiming that Jesus is the Messiah, writing individual books, claiming how other people, Jews, Pharisees, and Sadducees (who were religious leaders), saying that Jesus was demon possessed? And now they're expecting us to believe He truly was the Son of God? That doesn't make any sense. Why wouldn't they only tell us the good things when speaking about Jesus? I mean they are trying to convince us of His divinity, aren't they? The disciples even go as far as to say that after Jesus's resurrection, the women told the disciples His body was missing, and they had seen Him (Luke 24:11), and yet the disciples didn't believe them and thought of it as nonsense. Why wouldn't they write the story showing their faith in Jesus's resurrection and say they were the ones who ran to the tomb? At the crucifixion, all the disciples abandoned Jesus, except the women. Why wouldn't they have said that while the men stayed by Jesus's side, the women ran away in fear? Instead, the gospels tell us that the women were the ones with Him every step of the way.

All these stories are very embarrassing detailed testimonies! If anything, it would seem to have made them lose credibility rather than gain it. What man is going to write a story based on truth and admit that they were scaredy pants and ran away when trouble came? What man would say, "While we were scared and tucked our tails and ran, the women stood up and were brave?" It doesn't make any sense unless it was the truth.

To this very day, there's a story that is still circulated throughout Judaism about the resurrection of Jesus. Do you know what it is? The story that Jesus's body was stolen from the tomb to make people think He had risen from the dead. Is this an actual possibility? Yes, it is, but it isn't logical. Why? Because there is reasonable evidence pointing to this rumor not being true. For one, Jesus's body has never been discovered. Two, the testimony of the Roman soldiers who were meant to watch over the body to prevent theft would've most likely been killed for allowing that to happen. The eyewitness account of the soldiers would never have been able to sustain the test of time. How much sense does it make for the Roman soldiers to say that they saw His disciples (meaning, Jesus's disciples) come and take His body while they were sleeping? How can you see people do anything if your eyes are closed and asleep? That doesn't even make sense. Is it possible to prove that Christianity is false? Absolutely! How? By finding the body of Jesus of Nazareth. Finding the body of Jesus would completely and utterly destroy Christianity and prove it to be false. Christians around the world would have to come to the realization that they've been worshipping the wrong God—but considering after two thousand years they haven't found His body, and I personally know they never will, for He has risen.

As mentioned earlier a few chapters back, we are going to have to believe that Jesus of Nazareth was God/the Son of God before we can have belief in Jesus of Nazareth as being God/the Son of God. Many people have trouble with understanding or even believing in the Holy Trinity of the Christian faith. They like to say things like, "So what about that whole Trinity thing? I don't understand how there are three gods but only one God or how Jesus was claiming to be God and the Son of God at the same time? None of that makes

STAND FOR GOD

sense." This is a great question and also a great mystery even among Christians, scholars, and theologians.

The Holy Trinity is hard for anyone to understand. In fact, I say that if someone claims they completely understand it, I'd seriously have to doubt they do. The best way I have ever heard the Trinity explained was like this: Imagine you have a triangle. In the center of the triangle is "divine nature." At the top of the triangle is the Father, divine nature. Bottom left corner is the Son, divine nature but also the Son's human nature; and in the bottom right corner is the Holy Spirit, divine nature. So anytime you ask a question about Jesus, you actually have to ask two questions because you're dealing with two separate natures (divine and human). If you say, "Did Jesus get hungry?" His human nature yes, His divine nature no. "Does Jesus know when He's returning?" His human nature no, His divine nature yes. "Did Jesus get tired?" His human nature yes, His divine nature no. Now I'm not saying this makes knowing the Trinity any less difficult, but hopefully, it clears up a little less confusion. If you look up our YouTube channel The Christian Apologist, we have a video out there that gives a visible diagram of the Trinity outline.

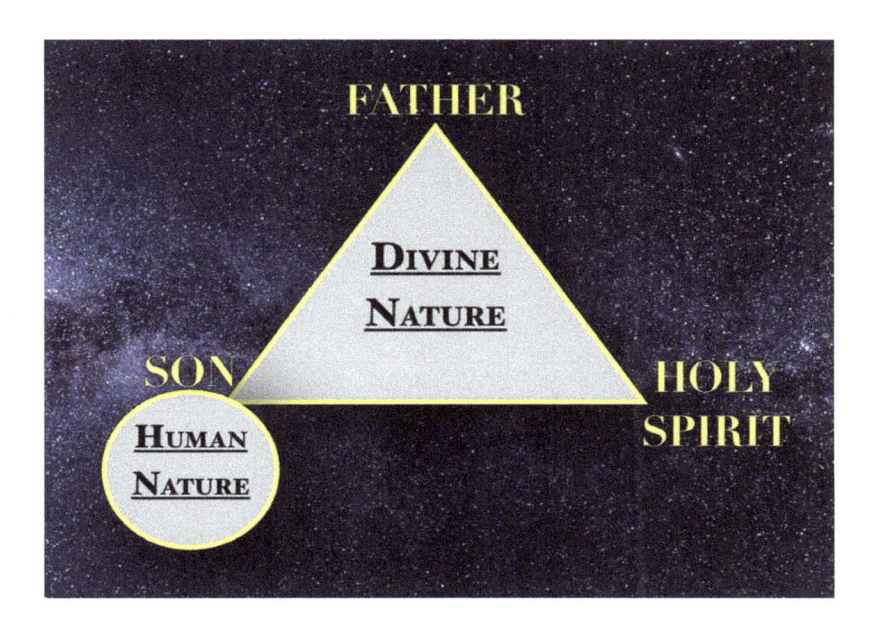

Do you know how many people claim to be atheist, or agnostic and have never read the Bible? Over half! How can someone claim to be the voice of reason and never have read the story of the most influential person to have ever lived? He is literally the central figure of the world's largest religion. I don't care who you are, what your beliefs are, if you have no beliefs, or if you don't even want to believe that Jesus ever actually existed (but even world-renown atheists don't deny Jesus lived), you are doing yourself a great injustice by not at least reading the New Testament. Why? Because either way, you believe or don't believe Jesus of Nazareth is unarguably the most influential person who has ever walked this planet. In 1926, Dr. James Allan wrote a sermon/poem titled "One Solitary Life." Here's what it said,

> He was born in an obscure village the child of a peasant woman. He grew up in another obscure village where He worked in a carpenter shop until He was thirty. He never wrote a book, He never held an office, He never went to college, He never visited a big city, He never travelled more than two hundred miles from the place where He was born. He did none of the things usually associated with greatness. He had no credentials but himself. He was only thirty three. His friends ran away, one of them denied Him. He was turned over to His enemies and went through the mockery of a trial. He was nailed to a cross between two thieves. While dying, His executioners gambled for His clothing, the only property He had on earth. When He was dead, He was laid in a borrowed grave through the pity of a friend. Nineteen centuries have come and gone, and today Jesus is the central figure of the human race and the leader of mankind's progress. All the armies that have ever marched, all the navies that have ever sailed, all the parliaments that have ever sat, all the kings that ever reigned put together,

have not affected the life of mankind on earth as powerfully as that one solitary life." Thomas Aquinas sums it up best "For those with faith, no evidence is necessary; for those without faith, no evidence is suffice.

The entire Bible can be summed up by only one word. Do you know what that word is? *Redemption.* Why's that? The beginning of the Bible has paradise lost. The end of the Bible has paradise regained, and everything in-between is God redeeming His people.

FINAL DESTINATION

Atheists don't worry about their final destination (eternal life after death). They believe once this life is over, you are placed in the ground or cremated, and that's that. But if God does exist (and He does), then how can God be so loving and yet also be willing to send His children to hell for all eternity? What kind of loving God does that? These are a few arguments atheists like to make about God. But the easy answer to this is, a God of justice that's who! It's hard for atheists and many Christians to accept this fact. God being all-loving and wanting nobody to perish is also a God of justice. For Him not to judge us righteously would be going against His very own nature.

When I first began doing Christian apologetics, I had a person ask me one time, "I'm a good person. I don't do wrong to anyone. I volunteer at different charities. I donate money. I obey the law, but I don't believe in Jesus. Are you saying you think I'm going to hell because I don't believe in this one man?" Wow! Talk about being put on the spot. My mind was racing. I've gone over this and over this and over this in my mind about someone asking a question like this, but now here I am in front of people, and I felt like I had been blindsided by a 350-pound lineman. I gained my composure and very respectively said, "What I think doesn't matter. I'm not the creator of all life. I'm not God, but what do you mean by you're a good person? According to whose standards are you basing being a good person from? Your standards, God's standards, Hitler's standards?"

They replied, "I'm good based on what society considers to be a good person."

I said, "Well according to the Bible, Romans 3:10 says that nobody is good. And in Isaiah 64:6, all good deeds are but filthy rags to God."

He then says, "Okay then, fair point. So is God implying that I'm going to hell because I choose not to believe in Jesus?"

I said, "Do you want to go to heaven after you die?"

He says, "Well I don't believe in heaven, so that question is not relevant to me."

I replied, "I can tell you this much. I don't know who is going to heaven and who's not going to heaven. I'm not the lawgiver, the judge, the creator, the designer, or the sustainer of life, and that isn't up to me. What I do know is that God loves you too much to force you into His presence for all eternity against your will. That's what heaven and hell are. Heaven is in God's presence for all eternity. Hell is the absence of God for all eternity."

He changed his stance and said, "Okay, well, what if I do want to go to heaven?"

I replied back and said, "Then why wouldn't you want to seek Jesus now?" After that, he walked away.

People need reasons to dislike God. They don't want God to be true. Why? By believing in God and choosing to accept Him, would convict them of all their wrongdoings, and they would be forced to admit that they are in need of a Savior. The rejection of God and/or Jesus isn't because they mentally can't grasp the evidence before them as plausible. Rejection of God and/or Jesus isn't because their brains can't comprehend it but because their hearts don't want to apprehend it. They would rather choose to see God as this moral monster. They want to think of God as someone who is constantly standing over us, ready to slap our hands and force us into hell. But that simply isn't the God of the Bible.

God loves all of us the same. He doesn't want to see anyone go to hell (1 Timothy 2:4). Hell wasn't made for us! It was made for Satan and his demons (Matthew 25:41). There are many people who are always ready to point a finger at someone else for their own decisions and their own choices. People reject God repeatedly, deny His Son who died for our sins; and then when confronted about heaven or hell, they claim it's God who's sending them to hell. What is sending people to hell isn't God or Satan. Why? Your sins send you to hell. Sin is sending every one of us to hell. The only reason we are saved from hell is by believing in the one who was sinless and has already died for our sins, the great physician (that being Jesus).

Let us suppose someone has a terminal illness and refuses to go to the doctor. Sometime later, that person dies from the illness. What killed them? Was it their refusal to seek medical attention? No, it was terminal, but it might have helped prolong their life. What ultimately killed them was the illness itself. Even though God wants all of us to be saved, He already knows many will not be saved. This doesn't mean He loves them any less. If people choose to reject God now and His free gift of salvation, then He isn't going to force them into His presence for all eternity. That wouldn't be very loving of Him if He was to do that. Dr. Frank Turek gives this illustration, "Have any ladies ever had a man who wanted to be with them, but the ladies only liked him as a friend? This guy constantly sends you gifts, buys you cards, sends you flowers, but you're just not into him like that. She finally tells him she only likes him as a friend. He says nope, I can't accept that. I'm going to force her to be with me until she does love me." Would she actually fall in love with him or despise him for forcing himself on her? Despise him, of course. Would him forcing her be a sign of true love on his part? No, more like creepy. Ladies, if this happens, *run!* If he truly was in love with her, what would he do? Like the old saying goes, if you truly love someone, you have to let them go. This is a great way to look at God's love toward all of us. He sends all of us gifts, flowers, and cards; but if we don't love Him back, then He leaves us alone. He loves us too much to force us into His presence for all eternity (heaven).

So why would God judge our sins all the same giving us all the same punishment? That seems kind of harsh, doesn't it? Yes, that would be harsh and unjust, but God isn't an unjust God. He is a just God. Punishment for someone who disobeys their parents wouldn't warrant the same kind of judgment as, let's say, someone like Adolph Hitler. We know that there's a hierarchy of sin. Most of us grew up hearing that all sin is equal. Sin is sin. It's all the same. But it isn't! Not all sin is equal. Really? Yes, really.

Look at John 19:11, Jesus says that "the one (being Judas Iscariot) who handed him over is guilty of a greater sin." The word *greater* signifies that there has to be sins that are of lesser value. Sin is still sin and is still subject to hell from judgment by God, but this verse tells us that the harshness of judgment will depend on the sin that was committed. Let's look at it from a different angle. My friend and I live in the United States. I live in one town, and my friend lives in another town six hundred miles away. There are many differences between our two towns. Restaurants are different, our entertainment is different, the town speed limits are different, and there's a ton of more things we could list about the differences between the two towns. But the one thing that remains the same is we are both still in the United States. Same is with hell. Although the levels of judgment might not be as bad for some as others depending on the severity of their sins, one thing remains the same. It's all still hell (the separation from God). If we have laws, judges, and degrees of punishments on earth, then how can we think the Creator of life wouldn't Himself be the standard of justice?

But what if God hasn't shown Himself to me? This statement doesn't work because God has shown Himself to the entire world! How? "Look up and see: who created these? He brings out the starry host by number; He calls all of them by name. Because of His great power and strength, not one of them is missing" (Isaiah 40:26). It doesn't matter where you are. By looking up at the sky, you can see God's hand at work.

What about those who have never heard of Jesus? This is a great question. Unfortunately I don't have time to answer it in this book. I'm just kidding. There are many people who died before Jesus was born whom we know are in heaven—for example, Moses, Abraham, Isaac, Jacob, Job, Elijah, Adam, Eve, Sarah, and the list goes on. None of these people knew Jesus or had even heard of His name. So how were they saved if Jesus said, "Nobody comes to the Father except through me" (John 14:6)? For those who died before Jesus came, we have to remember that God is outside the realm of time. Everything has already happened from His perspective, including the crucifixion of Jesus. So even in the days of the Old Testament, Jesus's crucifixion covered their salvation as well. The Bible also says that their faith in God was accredited to them (Genesis 15:6 and Romans 4:3). So by their belief in God and the realization that a Savior was coming was the same as them believing in Jesus since Jesus and God are one.

Now as far as people who have died after Jesus's resurrection and never heard of Him, I cannot be positive about this, but I speculate a few things. Just as the men and women of the Old Testament had their faith accredited to them and they went to heaven, I believe God would still do the same thing today. Now this other possibility is hard for some to accept, but it is a possibility nonetheless. God already knew beforehand when and where we would live (Acts 17:26), and He knew who was going to accept Him and who wasn't since He's outside the realm of time and all-knowing (omniscient).

How do we not know that the ones who never heard about Jesus wouldn't have believed in Him anyways? Is that possible? Yes, it's possible. The United States is the most Christian nation in the world (though at times, it doesn't seem like it). And yet we have people in the United States who are of all different kinds of religions and atheists and agnostics. Most, if not all of us in the US, have heard of Jesus, and many still don't believe. How then can we make an assumption that certain other people in far-off countries who have never heard of Him would have believed in Him? God is the standard of justice. Nothing He does can deviate from who He is. No matter where people might be located, God can get the gospel to them if He knows they would accept it and believe.

If atheists (being the voice of reason) would only admit that the possibility of there being a God is at least plausible, then it begs to differ why they wouldn't consider Pascals Wager. What's Pascals Wager? Blaise Pascal was a seventeenth-century French theologian, philosopher, mathematician, and physicist. This is what he has to say about choosing to believe in God, "If God does not actually exist, such a person will have only a finite loss [some pleasures, luxury, etc.], whereas if God does exist, he stands to receive infinite gains [as represented by eternity in heaven] and avoid infinite losses [eternity in hell]." All he's saying is if you choose to believe in God and He is real, you will gain heaven. If God is true and you choose not to believe in Him, then you've lost everything and have received eternal residency in hell. If God isn't true and you choose to believe, then either way you believe, you're losing nothing. That's a lot to consume. In even simpler terms, we can say this, "If God isn't true and you believe in Him, you lose nothing. If God is true and you don't believe in Him, you lose everything.' Yeah, that's much easier said.

There are some horrendous acts many people commit in their lifetime and get away with it, people such as Hitler, Stalin, other murderers, rapists. Sometimes the police can't figure out who did it or doesn't have the evidence to prove it. There are times our judicial system fails when prosecuting someone, and these people never have to pay for their crimes on earth. Are we to think that even after death, these people will not be judged by their wrongdoings? Hitler committed suicide. Stalin, after suffering a stroke, shook his fist toward God one last time before dying. None of these men ever had to face worldly judgment of the crimes they committed against humanity. How's that fair? If you're an atheist, you just have to accept that fact.

Being an atheist or being agnostic is a choice. You either can choose to believe in God, or you can choose not to believe in any God. Either way, you're having to believe in something. Why would anyone choose not to believe that these men or certain individuals will never be judged for the things they have done?

If Christianity is true (and it is), then none of us actually die. We just change locations. What do I mean? We either spend eternity in the presence of God, or we spend eternity in the absence of God. Our final destination is a choice we all have to make. God isn't going to force us one way or the other. We either admit that we are fallen beings in need of a Savior, or we don't. We either follow the evidence to the most logical, plausible explanation, or we refuse to follow that path because we don't like where it leads. And we sum all of it up to a lucky chance that the universe, the earth, and all of us are here today. Some like to say, "But if God truly loves all of us, then He wouldn't want us to be separated from Him." You're absolutely right! He doesn't want anyone separated from Him, and that's why

He sent His Son to die for us. He can't force you to believe it or to follow Him. What God did do was leave us a history book of all that has happened and allowed us the free will to either choose to believe it or not.

So what's wrong with spending eternity in hell? Well, right now on earth, Christians and non-Christians alike all get to experience a life covered under God's grace and His nature. How? We all experience love, joy, happiness, hope, truth, kindness, laughter, and justice. Without God's presence, we would have none of these things. Try to imagine a place that exists that is consumed with sadness, despair, hopelessness, anger, injustice, evil, dishonesty, and the people there are filled with nothing but narcissistic attitudes. Sounds horrible, doesn't it? That is what we mean when we say the US Senate. No, I'm just kidding. That's what we mean when we say hell. Are people really willing to play Russian roulette with their eternal salvation? Does not following the evidence to the easiest solution take less faith than believing in luck or chance?

WHAT THE BIBLE DOESN'T MENTION

If you have ever read the Bible, you know that the Bible doesn't tell us everything we feel like we need to know. There are many things the Bible never mentions specifically. Why? Wouldn't God want us to know everything we need to know by reading His Word? No. Why? The Bible makes it very clear that there are many things that are beyond our knowledge and beyond our understanding. "For my thoughts are not your thoughts, neither are your ways my ways declares the Lord. For as the heavens are higher than the earth, so are my ways higher than your ways, and my thoughts than your thoughts" (Isaiah 55:8–9). Also, in Ecclesiastes 3:11, "He has made everything beautiful in its time. Also, He has put eternity into man's heart, yet so that he cannot find out what God has done form the beginning to the end." The entirety of the Bible isn't to give us full knowledge of the world and everything in it. The Bible was written so we would know the origins of the universe, humanity, God's goodness, His power, His grace, His love, and how we get back into His presence. In fact, the majority of the Bible is written as a description rather than a prescription. The Bible, nor any book for that matter, can list everything about everything. The Bible is already a thick collection of separate books. What the Bible does do is help us to understand where we came from, and how to get back into His presence (heaven).

Many atheists, and surprisingly Christians, think that because the Bible doesn't specifically mention certain things such as dinosaurs, then the Bible is claiming that dinosaurs didn't exist. Well, to fellow Christians and atheists, I hate to be the bearer of bad news.

But the Bible does mention dinosaurs, and dinosaurs obviously did exist. How can we look at the bones of dinosaurs and make claim they never existed? That's ridiculous! Dinosaurs did exist! I'm at a loss of words if someone tries claiming they never existed. One can't possibly logically think and assume that Satan ran around making dinosaur bones and planted them around the world for us to discover later to only throw us off and confuse us. If they do, then I'm going to need to see proof for this claim. So where does the Bible mention dinosaurs? Job 40:15–24 speaks of the behemoth. Now some believe the description of the behemoth is of an elephant or a hippopotamus. It is a plausible explanation, but not a logical one due to verse 17. Verse 17 says this animal stiffens his tail like a cedar. Elephants and hippopotamus do have tails; but they are small, thin, and more like a soft spaghetti noodle. They are not like a cedar. The text points more to the animal being a Sauropod dinosaur.

So why doesn't the Bible just say dinosaur if that's what it truly is? Good question, but I can only assume it's because the Book of Job was written somewhere between the fourth to seventh century BCE, and paleontologist Richard Owen first coined the term *dinosaur* in 1842. So why wasn't the word *dinosaur* mentioned in the Bible? Because it wasn't a word in those days. There are many words that we use today that were not available in biblical days. Just talk to any teenager. It seems language changes every generation. Should we assume that these words don't truly exist? No, of course not! That would be nonsense. The word *dinosaur* is broken down into two parts and originated from Greece. The Greek word *Deinos* means terrible or fearful, and the word *sauros* is Greek for lizard or reptile. The Bible also mentions another "non-dinosaur" known in the Bible as the leviathan (Job 41).

If you really think about it, dinosaur bones help point to God's existence. How? Science shows us that dinosaur bones help point to the great flood of Noah's time. How's that? Many of the dinosaur bones that are discovered and have been discovered are found in mass burial sites. A major flood would account for this. In Canada, they found thousands of dinosaurs buried within one square mile of one another. In China, thousands of dinosaur bones were found within a

990-foot ravine. Even in the USA, mass bone beds have been found in thirteen states covering 700,000 square miles. There are even land dinosaur bones that have been found next to sea creatures (dinosaurs). How could that happen? How could land animals be found next to sea animals? We could assume that all the land animals committed suicide and drowned themselves. It isn't logical, but it is a possibility. We could assume that all the water on all the earth dried up, and all the sea animals died. That's another logical guess, but we have absolutely zero evidence to support that theory. The only logical analysis we have is of a worldwide flood. It's the only logical plausible way for this to have happened, even though Bill Nye (not a true science guy) claims the flood never happened. So how else would land dinosaurs be found next to sea dinosaurs unless the entire planet was covered underwater? Instead of the majority of scientist and atheist seeing the flood as a probability, they once again choose to ignore the logical evidence. But why is that? I tend to think it's either because it doesn't fit into their scientific agenda, or they don't want to admit that God could actually exist.

The Bible tells us exactly what it needs to tell us, nothing more and nothing less. The Bible is God's love letter to His children. The Bible reveals God to humanity, tells us about the fallen world, of our sins, and it tells us of Jesus's love to free us from our sins so we can be reunited with God for eternity. It's a warning of things that have happened and are going to happen. Simply put, the Bible is a love letter with the central narrative being redemption. There are many things written in the Bible that are hard to understand, but the reason for the majority of these is due to the Bible being written in the first-century words, and us living in the twenty-first century.

Some people ask, "Why did God wait so long to send Jesus?" And yet others say, "Why didn't God wait till much later to send Jesus so more people would believe in Him?" Once again, these types of questions can't be answered with certainty because the Bible doesn't mention specifically why Jesus came when He came. All we can do is use a reasonable deduction from the evidence we do know about. Many scholars and theologians believe that approximately two thousand years ago would've been the prime time for Jesus to have come into the world. Why? A few different reasons actually. At that time, the early Greek language was a universal language; so it would've been easier for people to understand, copy, and translate the manuscripts. Having a universal language easily helps people to spread news quickly and without misinterpretation. Also, at that time, the Roman roads were being built and the spreading of the news of Jesus could have easily taken off and spread across the known world quickly. Having a universal language and roads that could reach most civilizations quickly and easily seems to be a good reason for Jesus to come into existence when He did. Another possible reason is that, at the time Jesus was born and through the time of His crucifixion, the world was at peace with no wars. So let's sum this up, at the time of Jesus's coming, there was a universal language, easy roads for spreading the gospel, and world peace. Sounds like a great time to me, but I'm only speculating. This is by no means concrete evidence of why Jesus came when He did, but it's a good assumption based on the evidence of the events in that era.

Let's imagine what would've happened if Jesus decided to come much later, like in our time (twenty-first century) for instance. Good news: cellphone cameras are used all the time; so between the internet, social media, and the news, the Word of Jesus would've spread like crazy. Bad news: if He decided to come in the exact same fashion as He did in biblical days (i.e., poor, claiming to be born from a virgin, which by the way we would've called Mary crazy, and she would've ended up in a mental hospital or on the *Dr. Phil* show, which there was actually an episode of a girl claiming this, homeless, and claiming to be the Son of God), He would've been labeled a freak, liar, crazy, etc. Good news: Jesus could've prevented some wars we've experienced and possibly stopped COVID-19 before it got bad. Bad news: everyone would've concluded that all the miracles Jesus was doing were the act of a magic trick, science, luck, witchcraft, or chance; and He would've been most likely locked up for being crazy or demon possessed. Let's face it, we see magicians all the time on TV and know it's an illusion. Why would we believe some crazy guy claiming to be the Son of God born from a virgin girl whose now in a psych ward for believing she's the mother of the Messiah? Also, in today's world, there are over six thousand different spoken languages. Whose language would Jesus have used? And if for some reason some people believed Him, would they have translated the copies as good as they did in biblical times when most of the world was speaking Greek? It's sad to say, but I don't believe there would ever be a time frame that Jesus could've shown up, and we wouldn't have crucified Him. The only real difference between Jesus coming then and Jesus coming now is we would've gotten rid of Him a lot faster in today's society. Two thousand years ago seems like the best time for Him to have come. With using the logic that the Bible doesn't tell us everything and it should, then I'm guessing we all better stop cooking as well. Why? Because nowhere in the Bible does it teach us exactly how to cook. Oh, and we better stop driving or flying or riding trains also. None of those things were in the Bible either.

Claiming the Bible can't be correct or is a fairytale or that the Bible is misinforming because it doesn't say or mention everything about everything is completely ridiculous, and the logic behind it is utter nonsense. I suppose we all better stop reading any nonfictional books or history books if they don't tell us everything about everything in the world. Every book written is written for a designed purpose, and the Bible is no exception. It has a purpose, and it serves its purpose. The Bible, to this day, is the most sold book in the world. It's estimated that there are 100,000,000 Bibles sold each year. That is 237,972 sold a day, 11,415 an hour, 190 a minute, or 3 Bibles sold every second. Just because some people don't believe in God, Jesus, or the biblical stories doesn't disprove the existence of God, Jesus, or the biblical stories. To hold claim that something isn't true isn't enough proof that something isn't true. Atheists and other world religions making claims that Christianity isn't true doesn't disprove Christianity. Reasonable, plausible proof is needed to make those claims.

Christianity does provide reasonable, plausible proof for its claim that Christianity is true and, by deduction of the evidence provided, helps lead us to the most logical truth. If I say Christianity is true and someone comes along and says no it isn't, then I need them to prove their claim(s) to me. For me, to defend Christianity, I need some sort of evidence or proof; or I have nothing to refute other than their own opinions, and we've already established proof and persuasion aren't the same thing. When speaking of people from different religions or atheists, the first thing I want to know is if they've ever read the Bible or at very least the New Testament. I want to know why they believe Christianity is false. Most people make claims they have never actually studied but have heard from someone else or seen on TV or YouTube. I want to know how they came to that conclusion. I want to know if they have put in the effort to research Christianity for themselves, and if they have, how did they come to the conclusion that it's false? Following the evidence on almost everything we know about the Bible, science, laws, and theories, Christianity is the only plausible explanation. I want to know what evidence they have to provide for their claim that it's false. Reading books and making false claims is easy for anyone to do. For everything I say, I have evidence or a deduction of evidence that can point to Christianity. What is their proof? I also would want to know if they've ever looked into or considered the evidence provided for the truth of Christianity. How can a lawyer be a good attorney if they haven't looked into the evidence of the opposing attorney?

There's a great book on how to use these strategies to defend Christianity called *Tactics* by Greg Koukl. As a Christian apologist, I'm not here to make anyone become a Christian (though I hope they do), I'm here to defend the faith and hopefully plant seeds in hope that they research on their own and decide to see that the evidence provided for Christ does point to the Creator (God) and Jesus.

MIRACLES OR MAGIC?

The entire Bible is full of miraculous events. Miracles are recorded from the beginning of Genesis to the last book, Revelation. The miracles of the Bible weren't done randomly or done without purpose. The miracles in the Bible happened either through God Himself, a prophet, or a messenger of God. When somebody in biblical times was given a new revelation from God, miracles were a way to confirm this revelation. God used miracles as a way to get people's attention and to get them to listen to the person revealing the new revelation. Nobody would've listened to any of these people if they weren't able to perform some type of miracle that could confirm that the revelation given to them actually came from God. Even the miracles performed by Jesus were done as a way to reveal Himself as God/the Son of God.

Have you ever noticed that Jesus only performed four types of miracles throughout His life. The first miracle being that He was sinless. Second would be Him healing the sick. Third is Him controlling the weather/environment, and fourth rising others from the dead and Himself. These four types of miracles weren't done randomly. They were done for a purpose. All four types of these miracles were to show us what was needing to be fixed back then and is exactly the same problems we still have today. We're sinful, we get sick, we are harmed by natural disasters, and we die. The miracles performed by Jesus shows the world that He can fix all our problems. By Him performing miracles, He was giving us confirmation of who He was and why He was here.

When people question the truth about the Bible many times what they are questioning are all the miracles of the Bible. Some of the most talked-about and most controversial miracles are the ones such as the ten miracles performed by Moses to the Pharaoh, the great flood of Noah's day, Jonah being swallowed by a fish and then spit out three days later alive, Jesus healing the blind, calming the storms, walking on water, helping the cripples to walk, turning water into wine, and of course, His resurrection. The list of miracles goes on and on, but the ones I just listed are the ones I tend to hear most of the time from atheists and agnostics. What is strange to me is that people never really mention the greatest miracle of all in which we have scientific data to prove it. It's the very first miracle ever recorded in the Bible. Can you guess what it is? The creation of the universe out of nothing. Why doesn't anyone ever mention this miracle? Maybe it's because there is materialistic and naturalistic proof that the universe does exist, and so by admitting this, they would have to consider the possibility that all the other miracles of the Bible are at least plausible.

I recently had an atheist comment on one of my YouTube channel videos, and he said, "There is *no* credible evidence to support *any* supernatural claims in the Bible."

I responded, "There's plenty of evidence proving the existence of God. But are you looking for proof or persuasion? What do you mean by credible evidence? What supernatural claim are you referring to?"

He said, "*Any* supernatural claim!"

I then said, "Well, there's plenty of scientific proof that the universe exists, I'm sure you would agree to that, so I'll just use that one for my evidence for God."

After I explained all the evidence to show proof of God's existence through the observable universe, he never commented or replied back. If the universe out of nothing is at least a plausible miracle, then all the other miracles of the Bible are at least possible too. Most of the miracles mentioned in the Bible weren't seen by just one or two people but were seen by multiple people at the same time. The eyewitness accounts of these miracles cannot be dismissed because many of the eyewitnesses weren't even followers of Jesus. Like who? The centurions that were present at the crucifixion. These men helped crucify Jesus, and after He gave up His spirit, the curtain was torn. There was complete darkness for three hours, and there was a great earthquake (Matthew 27). One of them even commented and said, "Surely this was the Son of God." What reason would they have to lie? None, they wouldn't want to admit that they just hung the Son of God.

Scientists use science to look for causes. They are looking for some natural or scientific phenomenon that has to obey the laws of nature and/or physics and/or math and/or logic to come up with a conclusion as to why an event happened. They reject the idea of miracles because for one, miracles don't obey the laws of the world, and also, they have never seen one. So with this mindset, they are concluding that if something goes against all known laws and/or it only happens once, it cannot be true. Uhm yeah, that's kind of the point of a miracle. If miracles happened all the time, such as waters parting so people could drive through them or dead people constantly rising, it wouldn't be considered much of a miracle anymore, and Jesus's resurrection wouldn't have confirmed who He was. Miracles must be rare to gain our attention. There are many things other than miracles that break the known laws or sometimes only happen once, and yet, they don't call those things false. Like what, you might ask. Any time you toss a ball into the air, you're breaking the law of gravity. Also, today, for instance, only happens once. We don't call today yesterday or today tomorrow. They don't consider today to be a miracle, and it only happened once. The big bang only happened once, and scientists don't have a problem with that. We don't call it the big bang, bang, bang theory. By using the same logic scientists are using, then I guess we can say that since the big bang only happened once, it must not have ever happened. Sounds ridiculous, doesn't it?

I was once talking to someone about the miracles of the Bible, and they said, "How is it if miracles are only from your God that other religions who worship different gods also have miracles? Wouldn't that prove that there is more than one true God?" I'm going to be completely honest here. I have placed the majority of my time, energy, and effort into the studying of Christianity not because

I'm blinded by the fact of other religions existing but through my research of the evidence for Christianity, I have discovered it provides enough proof to me that Christianity (Jesus) is the one true God. I have studied other religions as well, but not to the extent of studying each miracle they claim. Miracles claimed by other religions would have to be studied on a case-to-case basis to verify their validity. Christianity and miracles are pretty much a packaged deal. But also keep in mind that just as the magicians in the day of Pharaoh performed signs in front of Moses, others can still do the same now.

So how can we tell if it's a magic trick or a miracle? We look to the Bible and can see that all the miracles performed were done to confirm a revelation from God (that's a miracle). If the so-called miracle isn't aligned with God's Word nor is it confirming a new revelation from God, then it's most likely a magic trick. If you accept Christianity, then you have to accept that miracles did at least occur. Why? Because the universe exists, and Jesus rose back to life. If Jesus didn't rise from the dead, then Christianity is false.

So why doesn't God still do miracles? If the main point of miracles were to give confirmation about a new revelation, maybe miracles aren't happening anymore because God has no more revelation to reveal. Since the completion of the Bible, there isn't any need for miracles to happen. Now God still can cause a miracle any time He chooses, and I believe He does, but it's also possible that the need for miracles passed with the closing of the biblical canon. I personally still believe miracles occur, but not as often or on such a large scale as they use to. Not only that, but many miracles that I think occur are usually written off due to science and technology. What do I mean? If there is a car accident and all rescue personnel say the person shouldn't have been able to walk away and yet they do, that's a miracle! Using the same car accident scenario, when they look into the accident, they find that a metal bar was right above the person's head, and that's what kept the car from caving in on them. Some will say it was by luck that the metal bar happened to land there, but I see that as a miracle.

Miracles weren't done to grow popularity. They weren't done to gain money or to show off. All the miracles of the Bible were done with intent, and purpose, so God could accomplish His primary objective. And that was to give us a revelation of what He was either doing, had done, was going to do, or to educate people on His plan for them. Others claim the miracles of the Bible were nothing but magic tricks used to fool people. Is that possible? Not in my eyes. I can't even begin to pretend that is a logical possibility. Why? How are the universe and everything in it a form of a magic trick? When is the last time you watched a magician or someone perform witchcraft and they called down fire on an entire city, and it actually happened like it did with Moses and Elijah? When was the last time someone performed a magic trick and resurrected a person after being dead three days? I don't think those questions will ever be answered.

When God used people of the Bible to perform miracles, it wasn't a card trick. It wasn't as if Jesus said, "Hey, everyone, watch me cut Peter in half and then make him whole again." Or, "Oh, hey there, Luke. What's that behind your ear? It's a denarius!" "Mary! Hey, Mary! Hold up some fingers behind your back and let me try to guess the number. Four! Am I right? You were holding up four?" I'm not trying to make light of the situation, but some things I can't even begin to comprehend the logic behind it. Common sense can go a long way. Is a DNA strand having a 3.2 billion letter sequence in perfect order not a miracle? A miracle, by definition, is a welcoming event that can't be explained by natural or scientific laws. How can you explain with scientific laws or natural laws how a DNA strand comes together in a perfect 3.2 billion letter sequence? They can have theories on it, but if they can't prove it, then they have to admit that it could possibly be a miracle. How can you explain the big bang out of nothing, creating the entire universe and everything in it with natural and scientific laws? Once again, theories of how this happened don't account for how it actually happened. If it can't be explained, then it follows as being at the very least a probability of a miracle.

Newton's first law of motion states that an object at rest stays at rest and an object in motion stays in motion. This means that if something is moving in a specific direction, it will continue moving in that direction until something stops it. It also means if something is at rest, it will stay at rest until something moves it. As the big bang exploded/expanded from a singularity, everything was spinning in the same direction. Newton's law says whichever way the rotation was going at the time of the explosion/expansion, it should continue rotating in the same direction unless something stops it. Without throwing in attempted theories which haven't been proven, why is the planet Venus rotating in an opposite direction to the other planets? Why are certain moons spinning the opposite way to the planets they're associated with? I know there are theories on this, but none of them be can be proven by natural or scientific laws. That means it is at least plausible that an intelligent, personal, powerful, spaceless, immaterial being (that being God) had to stop it and spin it the other way; and therefore, it is a miracle.

I heard a college student ask an apologist during a Q and A, "How come with all the miracles I hear people claiming they've seen, such as the sick healed, and the lame walk, has nobody ever seen a miracle that made a person grow back a limb? Can God not do that?" I believe God can do anything, but the question they were asking is more of a morality question than anything else. They are wanting to know if God's all-powerful and all-loving, then why isn't He growing limbs back on disabled people? I have an easy answer—I don't know. You might not like that answer, but by me or anyone else saying "I don't know" isn't an argument against miracles. Why God chooses to perform certain miracles over others is beyond me. I'm not God. I can't say why He does some of the things He does or doesn't do. I know whatever He chooses is best for us. We don't have to like some of the things the Bible says, why it says it, and when God chooses to do certain things.

If I'm being honest, there are many things I don't like about what the Bible says. I'd like to change some things in the Bible, but that isn't up to me. I'm not the creator and sustainer of life. I don't have the knowledge and wisdom God does. The Bible says in Isaiah 55:8–9, "'For my thoughts are not your thoughts, neither are your ways my ways,' declares the Lord. 'As the heavens are higher than the earth, so are my ways higher than your ways and my thoughts than your thoughts.'" Simply put, we have to put our trust, faith, and belief in the one who does know what's best.

I DON'T BELIEVE IN GOD, BUT I HATE HIM!

Not being able to understand all of God's wisdom is what I believe to be one of the biggest influences for atheism. How? Atheists claim to be the voice of reason. They look to science, materialism, and naturalism to understand what makes sense of the world around us, the universe, and their lives. Many atheists can't accept things happening that can't be explained by those three causes. They don't like to admit the possibility of a God who has created all, ordains all, and sustains all. Why? Many atheists don't want to imagine an afterlife where we will all be judged. It scares them (though most won't admit it), and they can't wrap their minds around the possibility of an all-powerful, all-knowing, and all-loving God.

Let's look at this through the eyes of an atheist for a moment. Imagine being eighteen and you committed a crime but was never caught (*all* crimes are considered capital punishment). You become a criminal on the run. All your life you've been running, avoiding the cops, avoiding being arrested. Despite running from the authorities, you ended up living a pretty good life, held the same job for fifty years. You volunteered at charities. Everyone thought the best of you. You're a great person, but then it happened. One time, you slip up and get pulled over. You're arrested and booked in to jail for a crime fifty years ago. Now you have to stand before the judge, shaking, worried, scared, knowing what sentence the judge is about to throw at you (the death penalty). That's a scary thought for anyone. Now take that same story, but this time, when you're standing before the judge, a man walks up and says, "Your Honor, I've already faced the death penalty for this man's crime. If he/she accepts my death in place of their own, you will have to let him/her go." So being an atheist is scary, but it doesn't have to be! All any of us need to do is accept the free gift of salvation and believe in Him (Jesus of Nazareth) as our Savior.

Like mentioned in the previous chapters, if you ask almost any atheist, "If Christianity was proven to be true, would you believe it?" And surprisingly 50 percent say no. For being the voice of "reason," that isn't very reasonable, is it? It's not that they can't believe it to be true. It's because they don't want it to be true. Why wouldn't anyone want Christianity to be true? It's virtually the only religion that doesn't require you to work for your salvation. There is nothing you have to do, can do, or need to do to earn your salvation. It's a gift! You literally just take the gift of salvation that is offered to you.

Atheists don't like when a Christian's answer is "I don't know" when speaking about life, the universe, and other debated topics. They want to know. They need to know. But God tells us His ways are not our ways, and His thoughts are far beyond ours (Isaiah 55:8–9). There are things we don't know, can't know, and aren't supposed to know. Why? It isn't because God is unloving but because He is loving, and He knows that our finite minds can't handle all that His infinite mind knows. If we knew what He knew, we would be trying to play God. There are people now that are extremely intelligent and are trying to play God. Many people, Christians alike, are all trying to play God. Imagine how much worse it would be if we did have the knowledge of an all-powerful, all-knowing being?

Christopher Hitchens, a brilliant man, wrote many books in his lifetime. The majority of his books that spoke against the existence of God could be summed up in eight words, "There is no God, and I hate Him." The belief in God isn't a difficult one for the mind to conceive. It's the heart that doesn't want to accept it. It isn't an intellectual problem, but a volitional problem. Through all the evidence, the most logical conclusion to the universe and life is God. The difficulty of believing in God comes from the heart. So why would people hate God? If you're an atheist, you can't hate something you don't believe in; and if you don't believe in God, then why hate Him? Deep down inside, we are all born with the knowledge of God's existence. It isn't that people can't believe in God. It's because they don't want there to be a God. Somewhere down the line, something, or someone happened causing a person to hate God. Maybe it was a tragedy, a death, or someone needed someone else to blame for their circumstances. Most of us can't understand why all the evil happens or "bad luck" happens, so they split one of two ways. One way is, they either choose to hate God, blaming Him, or they choose to not believe in God and search for other answers to please their own curiosity. I have a news flash for most atheists, and they aren't going to like it. If you hate God or even the idea of a god, you are not an atheist, maybe an agnostic at best, but that would even be questionable. Why? You can't hate something you truly don't believe in. That's like me saying I hate unicorns or leprechauns.

If you are an atheist, I do ask that you look into your life and determine why is it you truly don't believe in God. There are some people who claim to be atheists but truly hate Him because of what some religions have done—for example, the Christian crusades, the "mass genocide" spoke about in the Old Testament, the killing of many people for religious purposes. For one, they and I agree about most of those circumstances. I don't agree with the killing of anyone for any religious purposes. "But God killed people or had them killed in the Old Testament." When God kills someone, it isn't murder since He's the creator of life. God can't murder. If Christianity is true (and it is), then God isn't murdering anyone. He's simply changing their location. As far as humans murdering for religious reasons, well, that's just murder! But you can't judge an entire religious group by the actions of a few. Christianity is a good thing, but anyone can take something that is meant for good and use it for bad. It would be the same as a person using a wrench as a hammer and then complaining that a wrench is a bad tool. The wrench isn't a bad tool when used as designed. Same is with Christianity. Christianity is a good thing unless you use it for a purpose that it wasn't designed for.

This type of reasoning is exactly what's wrong in the USA. today. How do I mean? We've all seen the news about some bad police officers murdering unarmed black men. It's a sad tragic event that should never take place. We also see all the rioting and murdering of innocent police officers. We can't rightfully assume all police officers are bad because of a few bad ones. We can't assume all of Christianity is bad because of a few bad ones either. "Okay, but Christians are hypocrites!" is what some like to say. I don't know about you, but I've heard that a few times in my lifetime. When I first started being told this or hearing this, I would be offended by this and didn't know what to say next. Why? Well, because it's true. I am a hypocrite! We all are. None of us can hold to the standards Jesus tells us to. "Be perfect as your heavenly Father is perfect" (Matthew 5:48). Thanks, Jesus, like I didn't have enough to think about already, and now you're commanding me to be perfect? How am I supposed to be perfect when you've already said nobody is perfect? But it dawned on me that I believe that was the message Jesus was trying to convey to us all along. None of us will ever be perfect, so that is why we need Him as our Savior. So when I hear people call Christians hypocrites I agree with them. I usually respond with, "Yes, we are. We have room for one more if you want to join us." I know I'm a hypocrite! That's exactly why I need Jesus!

Richard Dawkins said,

> Do you really mean to tell me the only reason you try to be good is to gain God's approval and reward or to avoid his disapproval and punishment? That's not morality, that's just sucking up, apple-polishing, looking over your shoulder at the great surveillance camera in the sky, or the still small wiretap inside your head, monitoring your every move, even base though.

People like Dawkins know why Christians try pleasing God. It isn't for any of the reasons he says, and he knows it. We try pleasing God for many reasons. One, we respect and love the one who died for us to save us. Two, pleasing God is better for us because His ways are true, loving, and holy. God doesn't want us to worship Him because

He gets something out of it. He wants us to worship Him because it benefits us. If you go into any situation with the wrong mindset, you can find a problem with anything. Why wouldn't we live for God knowing how much He loves us? Richard Dawkins claims he doesn't hate God because he doesn't believe in a God. If that was true, why would he write so many books doing his best to disprove something that he knows doesn't exist? I don't believe in leprechauns, but I'm not going to write several books trying to convince others why leprechauns don't exist. In fact, I'm not going to try to convince anyone at all of things that don't exist.

Why are atheists so hostile to Christianity? If God doesn't exist, what's the problem? This isn't atheism! This is what we call misotheism. What's misotheism? Misotheism is the hatred for God or gods. It turns out that atheists have to constantly try to disprove God's existence and try their best to point out everything they claim is wrong and evil with God. Why would they do that? We're all made in the image of God. We all have the moral laws written on our hearts from birth, and they need ways to suppress the undeniable truth so that way the world continues to make better sense to them.

Christopher Hitchens wrote a book called *God Is Not Great*. For atheists to make their case against God, they have to attack God. Christopher Hitchens says he's an atheist yet, in the title of his book, admits there is a God, just not a great God. They can't simply show proof of why atheism is true. They can't provide evidence showing God doesn't exist. They have to hate God and belittle God to show why they choose not to believe in God. Does that make any sense? I have to prove to you why God is a bad God to prove there is no God? If there is no God, then why do atheists hate Him so much?

Studies show that there are, at any given moment, an average of five to seven hundred million atheists in the world. Why are so many people turning to atheism? This is going to be a hard pill to swallow for Christians, but we all need to look in the mirror. The person staring back at us, yeah, that's who's responsible, not just you but all of us around the world. Why's that? Hundreds of years ago, many Christian churches decided to shut themselves off from the outside world to separate Christians from those that weren't Christians. They kept to themselves, and to this very day, many of us still do that. When we finally decided to stick our heads out and see the world in chaos, with almost three-fourths of a billion people claiming to be atheist, and then wonder what went wrong. We went wrong! We didn't do as Jesus commanded us! We didn't go out unto the world and make disciples. We sheltered ourselves from the world. How do we, as Christians, keep the gospel to ourselves, not allowing others to see how true Christians are to behave and then point our fingers at those who don't believe in God? We shake our heads at the tragedies going on in the world, then have the nerve to blame others for it! This was our mistake, but it's never too late. I heard a preacher one time say, "It's time to leave the church." People were stunned by this, but what he was suggesting is for us to get out into the world, preach, teach, guide, defend, disciple, and speak the truth about the gospel. Why do atheists hate God? Because there is no one there to speak the truth and to defend Him.

WHY WOULD GOD CREATE SATAN?

Have you ever wondered why God created Satan to begin with? If God is all-knowing, all-powerful, and all-loving, why did God create Satan knowing he would sin? Did God make a mistake? Did God not know this would happen? All these questions are very good questions that many Christians and almost all atheists ask sooner or later. Let's answer each one of these questions independently.

Why did God create Satan knowing he would sin? First, we must understand that Satan was a cherub at one time. "You were an anointed guardian cherub, for I had appointed you. You were on the holy mountain of God; you walked among the fiery stones" (Ezekiel 28:14–15). Angels are a lot like us when it comes to having free will. Like we established a few chapters back, God wants His creation to have free will, so even the angels can choose to freely love Him and follow Him or not. Unlike us, Satan, as far as we know, didn't have a tree of knowledge to eat from to bring sin into existence. The Bible speaks very little about the fall of Satan. Isaiah 14 speaks of Satan's pride being the reason for his fall from heaven. If angels have free will just as we do, then some angels choosing to go against God was almost inevitable. Satan allowed his pride to overcome him, and because of that, he was banished from the presence of God for all eternity.

How could Satan have sinned being in the presence of God? It's only reasonable to think that God had to allow some kind of distance between Himself and the angels for them to have chosen to go against God. Satan and all angels are all created beings. That being said, they do not possess the same power and knowledge as God because they are created beings. All of God's creations start off perfect and blameless. Even Satan was blameless at one time according to Ezekiel 28:14–15. God doesn't create sin. He creates free will, which allows the possibility of sin to occur. It's through free will angels and humans have a choice, whether to follow God or not (sin). He must allow the possibility of sin to exist to have a free will/moral creation.

Why would God allow Satan to become evil? God allows all of us to do evil. We are all allowed to do evil because of free will. Intervening in free will isn't giving someone actual free will, but only giving off the perception of having free will. The perception of free will would be the same as having a dog on a leash. When the dog chooses to run across the road in traffic or do something against your wishes, you pull back on their leash. The dog doesn't have free will. It's just a false reality of free will. It's a delusion. Satan doesn't have the same power as God though. Satan's powers are limited, and Satan can't force us to do things either. Satan's only tool and only form of power is deception, lies, and temptation. Everything in life that is considered evil or sin is brought on by deception, lies, or temptation. Satan can't force you to sin; but he sure does make temptation, lie, and the deception of sin seem beautiful sometimes. Believe it or not, though, Satan does have some good qualities. What do I mean? Like us, Satan has mind, will, and emotions. Those are all good qualities God has given to us and His angels. Unfortunately, Satan uses his good qualities to perform evil acts and deeds. Think of it like how science is now. We can use science to better understand the universe and the things that are in it. These are the good qualities of science. But many scientists use those good qualities to try to disprove the need for a God (that's bad). We all have good qualities, and some people choose to do evil with their good qualities. If you don't believe that, you can just turn on the news at any time, and you will see the evil people commit with their good qualities. Just because God has given us free will and good qualities doesn't mean we all choose to love Him and do only good.

A. W. Tozer said, "The devil is a better theologian than any of us and is a devil still." Satan knows the Scripture. Satan hung out with God, and Jesus in heaven. He knows they exist, and He knows who they are beyond a shadow of a doubt. He knows them better than any of us do! But knowing God and following God are two separate things. James 2:19 says, "Even the demons believe and tremble." A. W. Pink, an English Bible teacher from the late 1800s to the mid-1900s, said, "As Christ has a Gospel, Satan has a gospel too; the latter being a clever counterfeit of the former. So closely does the gospel of Satan resemble that which it parades, multitudes of the unsaved are deceived by it."

The saying "Through pain and suffering comes triumph" is a very true statement. If we never experienced pain and suffering, then it would be a lot harder for us to know how bad we truly are and are in need of a Savior. If all we ever knew was good and blessings, then we wouldn't come to the realization that we need God. We wouldn't even try seeking Him!

Did God know this would happen with Satan? Absolutely He knew! He knew before He even began creating the universe that any being He created with free will, such as Satan, would sin, man would sin, and Jesus was going to have to die for our sins. He knew the beginning to the end. Look at the life of Jesus. In John 6:70, Jesus tells His disciples that one of them is a devil. At Jesus's last Passover (the last supper), which is recorded in all four gospels, Jesus already knew Judas was going to betray Him. Jesus knew Judas was going to be the one to betray Him from the very beginning, and yet Jesus still called Judas to be His disciple. Why would He do that? He knew that this was the only way to redeem us from our sins. Everything God does or allows is to fulfill His purpose.

So why did God create Satan knowing this would happen? Look at it this way. It's the same as asking a parent why they choose to have a child knowing they would act up, rebel against them, and make mistakes. The Scripture doesn't say this, but I believe it's under good speculation to say that if it wasn't Satan who had committed the actual first sin against God, it was only a matter of time before another free will creation did (i.e., me, you, or someone else).

The Bible begins in Genesis 1:1 saying, "In the beginning God created the heavens and the earth." Genesis 2:1 says, "So the heavens and the earth and everything in them were completed." What we know from this passage is that Satan and all the angels were created in this time frame. How long was that time frame before Satan rebelled against God is only an assumption, but it seems to have been within the six-day period of creation because Satan was here before Adam and Eve. We don't know the time frame from Satan's creation date to the time of his fall. It could have been days, thousands, millions, or billions of years. We really don't know since we already established that the word *day* used in Genesis doesn't necessarily mean a twenty-four-hour period. What we do know is once Satan was banished from heaven, he has been on an everlasting pursuit of vengeance against God, God's creation, and most importantly us. Why us? We haven't done anything to Satan. It's simply because we are the only creation of God that was created in His image.

Satan attacks us for two reasons. One, we are created in the image of God, and Satan wants to destroy anything and everything that resembles God. Two, Satan knows that God loves us; and since he can't hurt God personally, he attacks the ones God loves in an attempt to hurt God. God creating Satan was not a mistake. God knows how all things will turn out, so therefore, He can't make a mistake.

One could say, "Couldn't have God done something different instead of creating Satan?" No. Why not? God is omniscient. God is all-knowing. He knows all possible results. He knew which way was going to be the only way for Him to redeem us and to achieve His purpose. God doesn't live in time as we do, so He sees all of time, beginning to end simultaneously. Imagine how much worse any other way must've been, if the only way was for God to allow His only begotten Son to be crucified.

Have you ever seen *Avengers: Infinity War*? I'm a huge Marvel fan. Spoiler alert for those who haven't seen it: Dr. Strange, possessing the time stone, could see into the future and out of over fourteen million future possibilities, he could only see one possible outcome that would defeat Thanos (the bad guy). When I saw that scene, I couldn't help but think of if that's how God might view time. No, I'm not saying that God is like Dr. Strange or Dr. Strange is like God, but only in the sense that he could see all future outcomes simultaneously. Dr. Strange was able to go outside the realm of time and see the end. That's what it must be like for God. God being outside the realm of time is able to see all possible outcomes and determine which way would be best for us and to achieve His purpose.

So does Satan cause all the horrible attributes of the weather? Most likely not. Why? The Bible tells us why the weather is the way it is (i.e., tornadoes, hurricanes, earthquakes, tsunamis, floods, and all other natural-causing disasters are a result of us sinning). Look at Genesis 3:17, "Cursed is the ground because of you" is what God said speaking to Adam right after he had sinned. So not only are humans cursed with sin, but so is the entire world.

I heard someone ask one time, "Why didn't God just destroy Satan after he rebelled against God?" That's a very good question, and anyone who says they know for sure why God didn't is not being 100 percent honest. Why's that? The Bible never mentions why God didn't destroy Satan right after he rebelled. All we have to go on are speculations and assumptions. To me at this moment, I have three reasonable answers I could give other than I don't know, and that is, it could possibly be that created beings cannot be destroyed out of existence. Every living creature who has attributes of God never seem to get destroyed. The spirit goes on and on. Our spirits can obviously be kept at bay such as in heaven or hell, but they never cease to exist. They just move locations. That is one possibility. Another possibility is when a judge on earth sentences someone to prison, it's because that person should have to pay for their crimes. Maybe by destroying Satan, it would be as if Satan never had to pay for his sins (i.e., crimes). God is a God of justice. If those who accept Jesus get to spend eternity in heaven in God's presence, then why wouldn't those who don't accept Jesus not have to spend eternity where they choose to be? Lastly and the one I believe to be more probable is just because Satan is a sinner. The fallen angels are sinners, and we are all sinners, doesn't mean God doesn't love all of us. He can still love us and hate the choices we make. All three of these answers are only assumptions not based on any proof or biblical context. God is truly the only one who knows the answer to that.

Does God hate Satan? Once again, the Bible isn't clear on this, but I would have to say no, probably not. Why's that? I believe God loves all His creation, but I do know He hates what Satan has done, is doing, and is going to do. You've probably heard it said before. God hates the sin, not the sinner. Will Satan ever get a chance to repent and go back to heaven? Absolutely not. The Bible is clear where Satan and his demons will spend eternity. What about Jesus's sacrifice? Is Satan and the demons' sins not covered under Jesus's sacrifice? No. Why? Jesus's sacrifice wasn't for all of God's creations, but only for humans. Nor would Satan and his demons choose to ever follow Jesus anyways. They don't want to be in the presence of God for all eternity. If they did, they wouldn't have rebelled to begin with while they were in the presence of God in heaven. Angels who rebel (i.e., Satan and his demons) are not covered under the sacrifice of Jesus. Humans are made in the image of God, not angels or any other creation of God's. Also, it seems to me that the reason Satan and his demons won't be saved by the sacrifice of Jesus is because they have seen God, they've seen Jesus, and they were with God before the very first sin. Them sinning against God is of a greater sin. None of us have ever seen God or Jesus, so Jesus's sacrifice covers our sin through faith in Jesus. Satan and his demons don't need faith in Christ because they know Jesus and have seen God face-to-face. They don't have a problem believing *that* God and Jesus exist. They have a problem believing *in* them. All the angels, including Satan, and all humans have choices. We can either choose to love God and follow God's commands, or we can choose to go our own way. Satan knowing God exists, seeing God in all His glory, chose not to love or follow God, but to rebel.

Would sin still be on earth if Adam never would've taken a bite out of the fruit from the tree of knowledge? Who's to say? The Bible doesn't tell us what-ifs. I would say most likely so. Why? Because we all go against God's purpose and will for our lives almost daily. Satan and his demons aren't the only cause for all the sin in the world. We have to take responsibility for some of it as well. Why? Well, look at Adam and Eve. Satan might've introduced sin to Adam and Eve, but he didn't make them do it. Satan and his demons aren't running around forcing every one of us to sin against God. We are doing that ourselves. This doesn't mean Satan and his demons aren't causing a lot of the chaos and influencing people to sin, but they are not the cause of 100 percent of it. Us humans are pretty bad and evil ourselves.

In fact, it is much debated that Eve in the beginning had lied/exaggerated before she even took of the fruit from the tree of knowledge. Where? In Genesis 2:17, God tells Adam that he "must not eat from the tree of knowledge of good and evil, for on that day you eat from it, you will surely die." Now in Genesis 3:3, Eve is speaking with the serpent (Satan), and she tells the serpent (Satan) God said "you must not eat it or *touch it*, or you will die." God never mentioned anything about touching the tree of knowledge, but only eating it. After that, God comes to the garden of Eden and Adam and Eve hide because of their nakedness. Adam tries blaming God for his sin by saying in Genesis 3:12, "The woman *you* (speaking to God) gave to be with me—she gave me some of the fruit from the tree, and I ate." Did Satan force Eve to eat of the tree? No! Did Satan tell Adam to blame God for giving him a woman? No! Just by Satan simply questioning Eve over what God had said created enough doubt for Eve to exaggerate or lie about what God said, and the ripple effect of sin continues today.

The Book of Genesis also tells us that a Savior was going to come and would defeat Satan. Where? In Genesis 3:15, "I (being God) will put hostility between you and the woman, and between your offspring and her offspring. He [speaking of Jesus] will strike your head, and you will strike his heel"—meaning, Satan might attack Christ by striking His heel but doing no damage, and Jesus would strike Satan's head ultimately destroying him. Satan knows his time is running thin. Satan knows he will lose the battle against Jesus. In the meantime, Satan will continue to attack God's people, taking as many down with him as possible.

SHOW YOURSELF!

Why won't God just show Himself? That's the typical reaction for those who don't believe in God. Many say that for them to believe, it would take God Himself coming down and showing Himself to them. In fact, I did a podcast on our podcast channel the Christian Apologist with an atheist. At the end of our conversation, I asked him, "What would it take for you to believe that God exist?"

He replied, "God would have to show Himself to the entire world, not just to me because I could be hallucinating or having a delusion but show Himself to the entire world. But then I would have to talk to Him to see what He's about before I could believe in Him or follow Him." I hate to break the news to every atheist out there. But God did come down as a human (that being Jesus of Nazareth), and we crucified Him. I don't see why every few thousand years, Jesus would have to die again and again just so people would believe that He exists. But I don't think they realize what they're asking for. By God showing Himself as He is (not in the form of Jesus), they would die (Exodus 33:20). Why? God is holy, and we are not. God is perfect, and we are not. Evil and pure goodness cannot mix. Second Corinthians 6:14 says light (goodness) and darkness (evil) cannot mix. It would be like trying to mix water and oil. It's like saying I'm in a completely darkened room with a light on. It's complete contradictory and self-refuting. By God keeping His distance from us is for our benefit.

But what if that wasn't the case? J. P. Moreland says, "God maintains a delicate balance between keeping His existence sufficiently evident so people will know He's there and yet hiding His presence enough so that people who want to choose to ignore Him can do it. This way, their choice of destiny is really free." What if being in the presence of God in our human bodies wouldn't kill us instantly? If God showed Himself to us, would that cause unbelievers to believe? Many would believe that He exists, not necessarily in Him. But by doing that, didn't God just take away their free will and their freedom of choice? Someone can choose not to believe that something exists, but once it's shown to them, they really don't have a choice anymore because their free will to believe that it doesn't exist has been taken away from them. By God allowing His presence to be known but not seen gives people the free will on what they choose to believe. So ignoring the fact that if we see God's face we die, if God decided to reveal Himself, we would all lose our free will, and nobody would truly love God because love, by definition, has to be freely given.

Now let us take this one step further. Let us now suppose that by seeing God's face, it wouldn't kill us, and it didn't take away our free will. What would be the downfall now of God making Himself seen by humans? Yay! Everyone now believes in Him and worships Him now, right? Not necessarily. What do I mean? Two thousand years ago God did make Himself known to humans and came down in human flesh, who is named Jesus of Nazareth. Did everyone accept Jesus? No! Why not? The majority of people didn't recognize Jesus as the Son of God. They saw His miracles. They heard His sermons and watched His life for three years. For three years God revealed Himself to people, and many still didn't believe *in* Him. Was it because they didn't know? Was it because they couldn't understand His teachings? Was it because God, in human flesh, was too hard for them to grasp? No, no, and no! They didn't believe He was God because they chose not to believe *in* Him as God. They didn't like Jesus telling them that the way they were living and the way they were worshipping Him or representing Him was incorrect, and instead of accepting what He said and did as the truth and deciding to change their beliefs and lifestyle, they chose rather kill Him and silence Him so they could go back to what *they* wanted to do. How much worse would it be if Jesus claiming to be God came into this decade, performing miracles, telling other religions they were worshipping false gods and performing miracles? Many, many, many people would want Jesus either murdered, placed in prison, or put in a mental hospital.

Have you ever heard the saying, "Seeing is believing?" That is only half true. What do I mean? Believing in something comes in two parts—the mind and the heart. I think the saying should be seeing is believing *that*, but believing *in* needs to be of the heart and the mind. We can see examples of this in the Old and New Testaments. Where? In the Old Testament, God had made Himself known to Israel, and they strayed away worshipping and sacrificing to idol gods many times. After God had freed them from slavery in Egypt and they saw the signs performed by Moses, the parting of the Red Sea, the pillar of fire leading them, the manna from heaven to feed them, and water from a rock just to name a few, they still questioned, doubted, and multiple times refused to worship God. They saw His presence. They believed *in* Him, yet they still chose to go their own way. The Bible goes as far as to say that even demons believe *that* He exists, but they obviously don't choose to believe *in* Him with their hearts (James 2:19).

The Bible says to look to the heavens to declare His glory (Psalms 19:1). We can all look up to the sky (those who aren't blind) and see God's work. We can look at the universe and see His mighty hand. Us breathing is a miracle. There are signs literally everywhere for people to see God's work, His power, His intelligence, His wisdom, His love, and His perfect standard. Yet people deny His existence.

So why doesn't God just show Himself? One, by seeing God's face in our human bodies would instantly kill us. Two, it would remove our free will, and we would no longer be a free will / moral creation but robots. Three, He did come to us in human form (that being Jesus of Nazareth) so by us seeing Him wouldn't kill us. And instead of Him rightfully judging us, He loved us, and *we* wrongfully judged and killed Him. There's good news though. God does promise to return and call all those that follow Him to be in His presence (heaven) for all eternity. Bad news. When He returns, He will also come to rightfully judge those who do not follow Him and condemn them out of His presence (hell) for all eternity.

Everyone alive believes in things they cannot see nor can touch. Like what? Gravity. Gravity can't be seen, nor can it be felt, yet everyone believes in gravity. Why is that? Is it because we can see the effects of gravity? Possibly. But we can also see the effects of God and His work. So how come some can believe in gravity, but not God? We also believe in air. Air can't be seen, yet we know it's there. Claiming not to believe in God because you can't see Him doesn't disprove that God does exist. If the claim is you can't believe in Jesus because of the same thing, well, you should take that same mentality and say the same about George Washington or Abraham Lincoln or anyone who lived hundreds and thousands of years ago. The argument becomes a circular argument and shoots itself in the foot every time.

BEFORE SCIENCE WAS SCIENCE

What exactly is science? Science is the act of trying to gain knowledge of the natural and social world. In a nutshell, science looks for explainable causes. Causes are the purpose for science. Science looks for causes to things we don't yet understand. According to Aristotle, three men (Thales, Anaximander, and Anaximenes), sixth-century Ionian philosophers were the first to search for causes of natural phenomena. The word *science* comes from the Latin word *scientia*, meaning knowledge. This word wasn't introduced as the term we now use science until the fourteenth century. Though science still searches for unknown causes, many times the answers to these unknown causes are written in the Bible hundreds and some even thousands of years before scientists discovered them. Like what? The earliest known documents suggesting the earth was round was in fifth century BC. No, it was not Christopher Columbus. It was a mathematician named Eratosthenes in ancient Greece who proposed the earth was round and came very close to what the actual circumference of the earth is. It wasn't until much later that satellites were launched into space in the twentieth century before we could come up with the true circumference number of the earth. But before we knew the world was round, it was widely accepted that the world was flat or the world was sitting on the back of turtles or elephants (Hindu mythology).

The Book of Isaiah was written between 740 and 700 BC. Since the time we're referring to is BC, the larger the number, the longer ago it was. The Book of Isaiah 40:22 says, "God sits above the circle of the earth." Isaiah was written two hundred years or more before Eratosthenes proposed the earth was round. It also says in Job 26:7

that God hangs the world over nothing, meaning, the world isn't sitting on anything. It's just suspended in space. Either someone was just really good at guessing, or the writers had insight to some divine knowledge. Who knew the world was round and was suspended by nothing? The Bible had knowledge of science (the cause) over a thousand years before science was even a word.

Let us investigate more into some biblical knowledge that scientists like to claim as their own. In the 1950s, genetic testing became possible. They would count the number of chromosomes in cells. It was in 1986 human hair was first used to genetically identify a person. Scientists discovered that every single strand of our hair (not mine since I'm bald) has a different genetic code that belongs only to you. The book of Matthew was written around AD 85, and the book of Luke was written close to the same time around AD 85–95. Matthew 10:30–32 and Luke 12:7 both say that every hair on our heads is numbered. We can interpret that as meaning our hairs are numbered in sequential order (i.e., one, two, three, four, five, and so forth), or it could be speaking about the genetic numbering code in each one of our hair strands. Either way, we read and interpret those two verses we're having to make assumptions that can't be proven, but considering almost two thousand years after it was written, we have recently discovered that each hair actually does have different genetic numbers is pretty incredible, to say the least.

Follow me now as we're going to go back in time and look at one of the United States presidents, okay, not just one of the US presidents but the very first US president, President George Washington. George Washington was born in 1732 and passed away in 1799 at the age of sixty-seven. George Washington's doctors claim he died of an illness known as epiglottitis which is an inflammation in the mouth that stops you from being able to breathe. Years later, we know the true cause of his death. George Washington died from bloodletting. What's bloodletting? Bloodletting spans over three thousand years. In simple terms, bloodletting is the removal of someone's blood, hoping to minimize the infection in the bloodstream. Back in the late 1700s, medicine and medical expertise wasn't what it is today, and bloodletting was a common practice. They would either drain the blood through means of an IV or by allowing leeches to suck the blood out of your body depending on how bad the infection was. George Washington's symptoms came fast and furious after one night of horseback riding in the winter cold checking on his property. By the time the doctors arrived, he was in bad shape and leeches were not going to be a fast enough option, so they had to drain his blood manually through an IV. The doctors ended up removing roughly 40 percent of his blood. To put that in perspective, for those who aren't in the medical field like myself, when giving blood 8 to 10 percent of your bodies' total blood volume is extracted from you, 8 to 10 percent is enough to make people dizzy. They removed four times that amount out of a sick elderly man. This is what ultimately killed George Washington. George Washington died because they removed to much blood from his system. Why am I telling you this? In Leviticus 17:14, it says, "For the life of a creature is in the blood." Leviticus was written in 538–332 BC. That's 2,500 years or more before George Washington died. The Bible told us that life was in the blood. If only George Washington's doctors would've read Leviticus, they might have not thought it to be wise to remove that much of his blood.

Albert Einstein came up with his theory of general relativity around 1905. In that theory, it states that time, space, and matter have to come into existence at the exact same time for anything to exist. Did you know that the Bible even tells us this? Don't believe me? Read the very first sentence of the Bible in Genesis 1:1. It reads, "In the beginning, God created the heavens and the earth." It literally tells us time, space, and matter came into existence at the exact same time. How's that? In the beginning (time), God created the heavens (space) and earth (matter). I'm not good with math, but I do believe the Book of Genesis was written before Albert Einstein's theory of general relativity was even a thought. How come scientists aren't recognizing God for stating what's needed for anything to exist?

Off the subject, do you know why God said to use the stars as signs for things to come? It's the one thing humans can't manipulate! God wasn't going to give us supernatural signs or revelation from something that could be manipulated by man. He uses the things that no man can manipulate. That was an extra bonus at no extra charge. You're welcome. I'm just kidding.

Science has been around since the beginning of time although the word *science* hasn't been around very long. God is the greatest scientist of them all. Science and God are not at war, nor should they be at odds. Science actually compliments God. It is through science we can show evidence for God and Jesus of Nazareth being who He claimed to be. It isn't the science itself that refutes God, His creation, or His being, but the scientist who interpret the data. I read something the other day my wife had shown me, and it really stood out to me and truly summed up the science versus religion debate. "It isn't science that proves Scripture to be correct, Scriptures prove science is correct. The Scripture is always true and correct. It's the science that aligns with Scripture."

BELIEVE THAT AND BELIEVE IN

The word *faith* can be summed up as belief. If you have faith in something, you have a belief in something. Just as if you lack faith in something, you lack belief in it. A lot of people do not realize that there are two different kinds of faith (beliefs). What do I mean? We can believe *that* something exists, but that necessarily doesn't mean that we believe *in* that something.

Let me give you an example. Judas Iscariot believed that Jesus was the Son of God. But he didn't believe in Jesus as his Lord and Savior, or he never would've turned Him over to Pilate. The Bible tells us in James 2:19, "You believe that there is one God. Good! Even the demons believe that—and shudder." So just because the demons know who Jesus is and believe that He is God, they don't believe in Him. They don't put their trust, hope, and salvation into Him. I've spoken to many people, and have offended them when I tell them they're not Christians. They claim to be Christians. They throw the title out there as if they are, and some will even wear clothing or jewelry (i.e., cross necklaces). When I got to know them a little bit and tested the fruit of the spirit, it's clear that they weren't Christians at all, but religious at best. Religion isn't what's going to save any of us on the day of judgment. Believing that Jesus is God but not believing in Him is no better than the demons.

In today's society, we have become the generation of tolerance. If Christianity claims things are sinful, instead of upholding the Word of God, we water it down to fit into today's world view of tolerance so that way we don't offend people. Christianity is offensive! If the world looks at Christians like all other religions, then we aren't preaching the true gospel. Jesus wasn't tolerant. Do we not remember when Jesus was calling the religious leaders at that time a brood of vipers (Matthew 3:7) and comparing them to Satan (John 8:44)? Do we not remember when Jesus went into the temple and started turning over tables and whipping people who were desecrating the temple (Matthew 21:12, Mark 11:15–18)?

So why have we become more of a generation that falls into the belief *that* category and not the belief *in*? Simple. Following all the evidence we do know, it's easily proven that Jesus lived, God exists, and the resurrection did occur. With that information, it's easy to believe *that* Jesus is who He says He is. Yet with people being easily offended now, they don't want to put their trust *in* Jesus because of what Jesus stood for and claimed. They want the salvation that Jesus has to offer; but they don't want to pick up their cross, deny themselves, and follow Him daily like Matthew 16:24 says, "Whoever wants to be my disciple must deny themselves and take up their cross and follow me." This generation has become the generation of take, take, take; but when it comes to denying themselves and giving back, they'd rather sit on the sidelines in fear of offending people and fear of being attacked through either social media, court systems, and in fear of losing their jobs. What is even sadder is Jesus warned us of these days and even called these types of people lukewarm. In Revelation 3:16, Jesus says, "So, because you are lukewarm—neither hot nor cold—I am about to spit you out of my mouth." Jesus was referring to those that believe that He's the Messiah, but they never placed their faith (belief) in Him as their Messiah.

Recently becoming popular is progressive Christianity. What's progressive Christianity? In short, progressive Christianity are people who believe the Bible but twist Scripture to conform to their lifestyle and others so it isn't offensive to them. This is very dangerous. I tend not to see them as Christians at all because their view of God and Jesus are completely different from what the actual Bible teaches us. They are worshipping a false god. We need to become the generation that stands up, stands out, speaks up, and speaks out about all that Jesus stood for and be prepared no matter what to call sin a sin. Jesus said in Matthew 10:33, "But whoever disowns me before others, I will disown before my Father in heaven." Nobody should be willing to risk eternal separation from God over fear of being shamed, ridiculed, fired, embarrassed, or outcasted. Many preachers today preach a watered-down gospel in fear of offending people or losing attendance. And yet still, they count it as a win for themselves if they have a false conversion. What do I mean by false conversion? A false conversion is when someone outwardly confesses that they have turned from their sinful ways, accept Jesus Christ as their Lord and Savior, but their hearts never change. They get to the "believing that" phase but never cross over to the "believing in" phase. It becomes a volitional problem, not an intellectual problem. The mind can grasp the evidence, but the heart doesn't want to accept it.

FOLLOW THE EVIDENCE TO JESUS

After following the small amount of evidence we have provided, are you willing to follow Jesus? Evidence always points to the most reasonable, logical conclusion. We can choose to be like our atheist brothers and sisters and get to the end of the evidence and deny where it leads. We can wait and assume that as more evidence comes to light, it might feel our inner desire of not wanting there to be a God. As discussed in chapter 1, the universe had to have had a beginning, and almost all scientists and atheists now know this and aren't even an argument anymore. If something has a beginning, then there has to be a beginner; and that beginner has to be timeless, spaceless, and immaterial. This is what's known as the Kalam Cosmological Argument (made famous by Dr. William Lane Craig). The evidence points to an all-powerful, personal, intelligent, all-knowing being.

We later discussed morality. If morals have an objective standard, then the evidence for a universal moral lawgiver has to come from a being who has a moral standard above our own. If there is no objective moral standard, then only relativism follows. So now we have a timeless, spaceless, immaterial, powerful, all-knowing, personal, intelligent, moral being. This being has all the attributes of who we call God. If, at the very least, all the evidence from the universe being created is possible, then all the other parts of the Bible have to be at least plausible as well. Why's that? Because if we can look at the evidence of the universe being created and that being in itself a miracle, then all other miracles are at least plausible.

We looked into the evidence of Jesus of Nazareth being God/the Son of God. We know about all the testimonies given, the time frame they were given, and how the writers had no good reason to lie. Archeology facts prove that Jesus was a real man who did live, and the body of Jesus of Nazareth has never been discovered. Following the evidence to God doesn't take much faith when all the evidence points to only one logical explanation. When atheists and all other religions can follow the evidence and not at the very least claim that God and Jesus of Nazareth is a highly logical, reasonable probable possibility, then it isn't proof, reason, or truth they are seeking. They are seeking anything else other than God to be the cause. Whether the cause is they don't want to abandon the religion they grew up in or the religion they come to know as truth or they just don't want to know God, thinking that if they don't admit to His existence or claim that there is a God, they will somehow fall below His radar and never have to face Him in this life or the afterlife. I don't know. The sad part to me is that everyone born has a God-given conscience.

We all know that God exists. Some can deny Him all day long and never once utter the words that He even might exist, but His existence isn't based on what we find to be true and false. The evidence for God and Jesus isn't based on what we think, what we believe, or how we feel. That reminds me, how many times have you heard people say that they just don't feel close to God today or they don't feel like Jesus is near, then all of a sudden, they start to doubt the existence of God and/or Jesus? What's changed? Has God changed? Has the evidence changed? No. They've changed! Their feelings changed. Our feelings change multiple times a day. God, Jesus, and the evidence never change. Just because someone who was once a Christian now doubts the existence of God doesn't change the facts of the evidence. The evidence we've provided is based on scientific facts, natural laws, morality, and philosophy. Those scientific facts lead to God and Jesus as the Creator, the Sustainer, the Lord of lords, the Redeemer of life, Yahweh, the great I Am!

ABOUT THE AUTHOR

Richard is a Christian apologist. An apologist isn't an apology for Christianity but rather a defense for Christianity. The word *apologist* derives from the Greek word *apologia*, meaning to speak a defense. The apostle Paul says in 1 Peter 3:15, "But in your hearts revere Christ as Lord. Always be prepared to give a defense 'apologia' to everyone who asks you to give the reason for the hope that you have. But do this with gentleness and respect." Richard is a gifted writer and speaker who is in continuous pursuit of the truth in finding evidence for God's existence and claims that a man, Jesus of Nazareth, was who He claimed to be the Son of God. Richard is an ordained minister who has a theology certificate from Gordon Conwell Theological Seminary, a certificate for Christian apologetics from Biola University, and endless hours of research and studying in philosophy, world religions, apologetics, ancient Hebrew and Greek writings, and Scripture. Richard's goal in life is to help other Christians defend their faith in Christ Jesus and to put a rock in the shoe of non-Christians to get them thinking about what is the truth. You can find more about Richard and apologetics on his Podcast channel and YouTube channel titled The Christian Apologist. Richard's favorite quote is "God exists. Prove me wrong."

Printed in the USA
CPSIA information can be obtained
at www.ICGtesting.com
LVHW071939010823
753724LV00016B/690